handy homework helper

English

study reference guide

handy homework helper

English

Writer:
Lynne Blanton, Ph.D.

Consultant:
Dorothy F. King, Ed.D.

Publications International, Ltd.

Lynne Blanton, Ph.D., is a writer and editor with Creative Services, Inc. She has served as editor for both Rand McNally and Riverside Publishing Company and has a B.A. in English and History and a Ph.D. in Communications.

Dorothy F. King is an Associate Professor of Early Childhood Education at the University of New Mexico-Gallup and has served as Chair for the National Council of Teachers of English Commission on Curriculum.

Illustrations: Chris Reed

Copyright ©2005 Publications International, Ltd. All rights reserved. This book may not be reproduced or quoted in whole or in part by any means whatsoever without written permission from:

Louis Weber, CEO
Publications International, Ltd.
7373 North Cicero Avenue
Lincolnwood, Illinois 60712

Permission is never granted for commercial purposes.

Manufactured in China.

8 7 6 5 4 3 2 1

ISBN: 0-7853-1953-0

Contents

About This Book • 4

English and You • 5

Part 1: Grammar • 6
    1. Sentences • 7
    2. Nouns • 16
    3. Verbs • 23
    4. Pronouns • 36
    5. Adjectives • 47
    6. Adverbs • 54
  7. Prepositions, Conjunctions & Interjections • 60

Part 2: Mechanics • 71
    8. Capitalization • 72
    9. Punctuation • 79

Part 3: Writing • 95
    10. The Writing Process • 96
    11. Skills for Writing • 117

Index • 124

About This Book

Homework takes time and a lot of hard work. Many students would say it's their least favorite part of the school day. But it's also one of the most important parts of your school career because it does so much to help you learn. Learning gives you knowledge, and knowledge gives you power.

Homework gives you a chance to review the material you've been studying so you understand it better. It lets you work on your own, which can give you confidence and independence. Doing school work at home also gives your parents a way to find out what you're studying in school.

Everyone has trouble with their homework from time to time, and *Handy Homework Helper: English* can help you when you run into a problem. This book was prepared with the help of educational specialists. It offers quick, simple explanations of the basic material that you're studying in school. If you get stuck on an idea or have trouble finding some information, *Handy Homework Helper: English* can help clear it up for you. It can also help your parents help you by giving them a fast refresher course in the subject.

This book is clearly organized by the topics you'll be studying in English. A quick look at the Table of Contents will tell you which chapter covers the area you're working on. You can probably guess which chapter includes what you need and then flip through the chapter until you find it. For even more help finding what you're looking for, look up key words related to what you're studying in the Index. You might find material faster that way, and you might also find useful information in a place you wouldn't have thought to look.

Remember that different teachers and different schools take different approaches to teaching English. For that reason, we recommend that you talk with your teacher about using this homework guide. You might even let your teacher look through the book so he or she can help you use it in a way that best matches what you're studying at school.

English and You

You are already an accomplished user of the English language. After all, you speak and write English all the time, and people understand you. But sometimes you may need to know more about the language or be reminded of what you already know. This book contains information on grammar, mechanics, and writing that you can use whenever you think you need it. It's a reference tool that can help you when you are completing assignments for English or any other topic that requires writing.

The dialect used in the *Handy Homework Helper: English* is Standard English. A dialect is a specific version of a language. People who speak different dialects understand each other, but they might use different words for some things. There are many different dialects in English. Everyone uses a dialect, and no dialect is "bad." But Standard English has one major advantage: It is the dialect used by people with political, economic, and social power. By learning Standard English, you increase your own possibilities for success in our society.

This book has three parts: Grammar, Mechanics, and Writing. "Grammar" covers sentences and parts of speech—the basic building blocks of the English language. "Mechanics" explains the rules governing capitalization and punctuation in English. "Writing" explains the stages of the writing process and discusses skills related to writing, such as using a dictionary or a thesaurus and remembering how to spell words.

Like a dictionary, thesaurus, or any other reference source, *Handy Homework Helper: English* is meant to be one of many tools available to you— a tool that you decide when and how to use.

Grammar

The main point of language is to communicate meaning. A person is judged by the skill with which he or she communicates meaning in speech or writing. Grammar is one tool for getting your meaning across. Grammar describes the way the English language works.

You already know a lot about English grammar. With practice, using the grammar of Standard English will become a habit, something you do not even think about. And when you use grammar correctly, you communicate your thoughts clearly.

Usually, we listen to what people say, not how they say it. But if they do not use language and grammar well, we may be distracted from the what by the how. To make sure people pay attention to what you are saying (or writing), you must use grammar and your other language tools to communicate clearly.

This section explains everything from sentences to parts of speech. You will find plenty of examples to give you a feeling for how to use these constructions or words in your own writing. Learning to identify parts of speech is important, but even more important is learning to use them to improve your writing. For example, you can use nouns to make your writing more precise, adjectives to make it more vivid, and pronouns to avoid repeating yourself. Learning to use parts of speech correctly will also help you avoid confusing and distracting your readers. Remember, you want them to concentrate on *what* you are saying, not *how* you are saying it.

Sentences

What Is a Sentence?

A **sentence** is a group of words that expresses a complete thought or idea.

>The band has a rehearsal at 1:00.

This group of words is a sentence. It expresses a complete thought.

Is this group of words a sentence?

>The children in the band

The group of words tells about children in a band. But the words do not tell what the children are doing or what happens to them. The group of words does not express a complete thought, so it is not a sentence.

>Practiced all afternoon

This group of words tells about something that happened. But the words do not tell who or what practiced all afternoon. The group of words does not express a complete thought, so it is not a sentence.

A sentence tells what or whom the sentence is about. A sentence tells about something that happens.

>The children in the band practiced all afternoon.

A sentence can be very long or very short. A group of words that is not a sentence can be very long.

>Jane called.

>Running through the field and feeling the warm sun

Even though it is short, the first example is a sentence, because it expresses a complete thought. Even though it is long, the second example is not a sentence, because it does not express a complete thought.

8 • Sentences

Subjects and Predicates

A sentence has two parts: a subject and a predicate.

The **subject** of a sentence tells who or what the sentence is about.

> **Clarice's dog, Randall,** is a small, gray terrier.
>
> **The dogs in the neighborhood** began to bark.

The **predicate** of a sentence tells what the subject is or what the subject does.

> Clarice's dog, Randall, **is a small, gray terrier.**
>
> All the dogs in the neighborhood **began to bark.**

Every sentence can be divided into a subject and a predicate, and every word in a sentence is part of either the subject or the predicate.

Subject	Predicate
Thomas	gets up from the dinner table.
He	takes the dishes to the sink.
His dad	usually washes the dishes.
It	is Thomas's turn tonight.
Washing dishes	is not his favorite chore.
His sister Marie	offers to help him.

Usually, the subject is at or near the beginning of a sentence, and the predicate is at the middle or near the end of a sentence. But this may not be true in some sentences. Always ask the questions "Who or what is the sentence about?" and "What is the subject, or what is the subject doing?" to identify the subject and predicate of a sentence.

See page 15 for information on subjects in different locations in sentences.

Sentence Fragments and Run-on Sentences

Both sentence fragments and run-on sentences are confusing to readers. Sentence fragments are confusing because they leave out important information. Run-on sentences are confusing because they connect thoughts that should not be connected.

Sentence Fragments

A **sentence fragment** is a group of words that does not express a complete thought. It is only a part, or a *fragment*, of a sentence.

A fragment may have a subject but no predicate. It may have a predicate but no subject.

> During the storm, the tree in the yard.
>
> Covered the floor and everything on it.

To correct a sentence fragment, add whichever part is missing and make the fragment into a complete sentence.

> During the storm, the tree in the yard blew over and landed on the house.
>
> In the basement, mud and water covered the floor and everything on it.

Run-on Sentences

Two or more sentences written as though they were one sentence are called a **run-on sentence.** One sentence "runs on" into the next sentence.

There may be no end punctuation mark separating the first sentence from the second. A comma may be used incorrectly to separate the first sentence from the second.

> The rain poured down four inches fell in an hour.
>
> The rain poured down, four inches fell in an hour.

To correct a run-on sentence, add an end punctuation mark at the end of the first sentence. Capitalize the first word of the second sentence.

> The rain poured down. Four inches fell in an hour.

Simple Subjects and Predicates

Remember, a sentence can be divided into two parts: the subject and the predicate.

Subject **Predicate**
The small, gray cat   ran under the bed.

The subject part of the example sentence is the **complete subject.** The complete subject is all the words that tell who or what the sentence is about. *The small, gray cat* is the complete subject of the example sentence.

The predicate part of the example sentence is the **complete predicate.** The complete predicate is all the words that tell what the subject is or what the subject does. *Ran under the bed* is the complete predicate of the example sentence.

Simple Subjects

The **simple subject** is the principal or most important word in the complete subject.

Look at these sentences:

Complete Subject **Complete Predicate**
The small, gray cat   ran under the bed.
The door of the house   shut with a bang.
A girl with dark hair   stood at the window.

The most important word in the complete subject in the first sentence is *cat*. In the second sentence it's *door* and in the third sentence it's *girl*. These are the simple subjects.

To find the simple subject of a sentence, first find the predicate and then add *who* or *what*. Who ran under the bed? (cat) What shut with a bang? (door) Who stood at the window? (girl) The answer tells the simple subject.

Simple Predicates

The **simple predicate,** also called the **verb,** is the most important word in the complete predicate.

Look at these sentences:

Complete Subject **Complete Predicate**
The big, black dog   howled at the moon.
One lone owl   sat in a tree.

The most important word in the complete predicate in the first sentence is *howled.* In the second sentence it's *sat.* These are the simple predicates, or verbs.

There are two kinds of verbs: action and state-of-being (or linking).

Action verbs express, or tell about, an action.

>Calvin **jumped** into the pool.
>He **swam** from one end to the other.

State-of-being verbs, which are also called **linking verbs,** express a state or condition. They link the subject to words that describe or identify it.

>The water in the pool **is** cool and blue.
>The afternoon sun **feels** warm.

The most common linking verb is the verb *be* in all its forms: *am, is, are, was, were, be, been, being.*

Other Common Linking Verbs

appear	get	remain
sound	become	grow
seem	stay	feel
look	smell	taste

Some linking verbs can also be action verbs. *Smell* is an action verb in a sentence such as *Marika smells the flowers.*

See page 23 for information on action and linking verbs.

Compound Subjects and Predicates

The word *compound* comes from two Latin words meaning "to put together." A compound word is made by putting two or more smaller words together. So what would a compound subject or a compound predicate be?

Compound Subjects

A **compound subject** is made up of two or more subjects.

Subject	Predicate
Joanna and Paul	like to play board games.
Chess and checkers	are two of their favorites.

Both example sentences have compound subjects. That is, they each have two subjects: *Joanna* and *Paul, chess* and *checkers*. The two subjects are joined by the conjunction *and*. A **conjunction** is a word that joins words or groups of words. Compound subjects may also be joined by the conjunction *or*.

Look at these sentences:

Joanna, Paul, and Maria belong to a chess club.
Men, women, and children play chess there.

These sentences have compound subjects made up of three subjects. Commas are used to separate the subjects, and the conjunction appears before the last subject.

Why are compound subjects useful? By putting similar ideas together in sentences, writers organize their thoughts and make their writing smoother.

Here are some examples of how you can put subjects together.

Chess is a very old game.
Checkers is a very old game.
Chess and checkers are very old games.

Joanna and Paul are good chess players.
Maria is a good chess player.
Joanna, Paul, and Maria are good chess players.

Sentences • 13

Compound Predicates

A **compound predicate** is made up of two or more predicates.

Subject	Predicate
Paul	**calls Joanna** and **asks her to come over.**
He	**clears the table** and **sets up the game.**

Both example sentences have compound predicates. That is, they each have two predicates. The two predicates are joined by the conjunction *and*.

Look at this sentence:

> The chess player **looked at the clock, studied the board,** and **made her move.**

This sentence has a compound predicate made up of three predicates. Commas are used to separate the predicates, and the conjunction appears before the last predicate.

Why are compound predicates useful? By putting similar ideas together in sentences, writers organize their thoughts and make their writing smoother. Look at these examples of how you can combine predicates.

> Paul won the first game.
> Paul lost the second game.
> Paul won the first game
> and lost the second game.

> They set up the pieces again.
> They played another game.
> They set up the pieces again
> and played another game.

See pages 66–67 for information on conjunctions and page 84 for information on punctuating nouns and verbs in a series.

Kinds of Sentences

Depending on what its purpose is, a sentence is one of four kinds: declarative, interrogative, imperative, or exclamatory.

A **declarative sentence** makes a statement.

> I saw a hippopotamus at the zoo.
> It was submerged in a large pond.

A declarative sentence ends with a period.

An **interrogative sentence** asks a question.

> What in the world is an okapi?
> Did you see a rhinoceros?

An interrogative sentence always ends with a question mark.

An **imperative sentence** gives a command or makes a request.

> Don't frighten the monkeys.
> Show me the way to the walrus, please.

An imperative sentence ends with a period.

An **exclamatory sentence** expresses strong feeling.

> Watch how fast the penguins can swim!
> What a beautiful color the flamingos are!

An exclamatory sentence ends with an exclamation point.

Some sentences can be one kind or another. For example, *Look at me* can be either imperative (Look at me.) or exclamatory (Look at me!). *You will* can be either declarative (You will.) or interrogative (You will?). It depends on what meaning the writer intends. The meaning is indicated by the punctuation mark the writer chooses to use.

Where Is the Subject?

In a declarative sentence, the subject is usually found at or near the beginning. But sometimes writers place the subject in other locations.

>Aliens from outer space appeared in the movie.
>In the movie, aliens from outer space appeared.
>In the movie appeared aliens from outer space.

To find the subject of a declarative sentence, find the verb and add *who* or *what*.

>Who or what appeared? aliens
>*Aliens* is the subject.

In sentences beginning with *here* or *there,* the subject usually comes after the verb.

>There are our seats.　　　Here is the popcorn.
>Who or what are? seats　　Who or what is? popcorn
>*Seats* is the subject.　　*Popcorn* is the subject.

To find the subject of an interrogative sentence, change it to a declarative sentence, then find the verb, and ask *who* or *what*.

>Did Sean watch the movie?
>Sean did watch the movie.
>Who did watch? Sean
>*Sean* is the subject.

To find the subject of an exclamatory sentence, change it to a declarative sentence, then find the verb, and ask *who* or *what*.

>Wow, was that movie scary!
>That movie was scary.
>What was? movie
>*Movie* is the subject.

Where is the subject in this imperative sentence?

>Wait for me outside the theater.
>Who should wait? you

Even though *you* does not appear in the sentence, it is understood to be the subject.

Nouns

What Is a Noun?

A **noun** names a person, a place, a thing, or an idea.

Everything has a name. Often something may have more than one name. A house is not just a house; it is also a building, a home, and a place. A woman is not just a woman; she may also be a doctor, a mother, and a golfer. All these words—*house, building, home, place, woman, doctor, mother, golfer*—are nouns.

A noun can name something that can be seen or touched, such as *tree, city, child,* and *star.* A noun can also name something that cannot be seen or touched, such as *laughter, greed, joy,* and *pain.*

Here are some more nouns:

Persons	Places	Things	Ideas
artist	farm	shirt	liberty
Chandra	Egypt	Great Wall	despair
student	continent	horse	humor
Darrell	Boston	Taj Mahal	happiness

A noun can be very general *(person, place, thing),* or it can be more specific *(boy, town, book).* Try to use more specific nouns in place of general nouns. It will help make your writing clearer and more precise. Compare these two sets of sentences:

The **boat** floated on the **water.**
The **animal** scampered up the **tree.**

The **canoe** floated on the **lake.**
The **squirrel** scampered up the **oak.**

The more specific nouns in the second set of sentences give the reader better, more detailed descriptions.

Common and Proper Nouns

A **common noun** names a general type of person, place, thing, or idea.

A dog may be a poodle, but so are a lot of other dogs. Because *poodle* is a name that can be applied to many dogs, it is a common noun. Common means "belonging to or shared by all alike." Other common nouns are *man, town, country,* and *building.*

A **proper noun** names a particular person, place, thing, or idea.

A dog may share the common noun *poodle* with many other dogs, but each dog also has a particular name, a name that is specific to it and to no other dog, such as *Jack, Flip,* or *Lady.* These names are proper nouns. Other proper nouns are *David Chang, New York, Japan,* and *White House.*

Proper nouns are always capitalized. Common nouns are not capitalized.

Here are some more examples of common and proper nouns:

Common Nouns	Proper Nouns
boy	Malcolm Ortiz
girl	Holly Jacobson
town	Des Moines
country	China
building	Sears Tower
ocean	Arctic Ocean
event	World War II
street	Maple Street
monument	Jefferson Memorial
newspaper	*The New York Times*

See pages 72–75 for information on capitalizing proper nouns.

Nouns

Singular and Plural Nouns

A **singular noun** names one person, place, thing, or idea.

When a noun names only one person, place, thing, or idea, it is a singular noun. *Singular* means "being one, separate, individual." *Boy* names one person. *Hat* names one thing. *Boy* and *hat* are both singular nouns.

A **plural noun** names more than one person, place, thing, or idea.

When a noun names more than one person, place, thing, or idea, it is a plural noun. *Plural* comes from a Latin word that means "more." *Boys* names more than one boy. *Hats* names more than one hat. *Boys* and *hats* are both plural nouns.

Plurals of nouns are formed in several different ways.

1. Add *-s* to form the plurals of most nouns.

| town | towns | dog | dogs | word | words |
| book | books | girl | girls | idea | ideas |

2. Add *-es* to form the plurals of nouns that end in *s, sh, ch,* or *x*.

gas	gases	dish	dishes	match	matches
bus	buses	brush	brushes	box	boxes
dress	dresses	bench	benches	tax	taxes

3. When a noun ends in a consonant followed by *y,* change the *y* to *i* and add *-es* to form the plural.

| penny | pennies | city | cities | enemy | enemies |
| baby | babies | fly | flies | story | stories |

When a noun ends in a vowel followed by *y*, add -*s* to form the plural.

  essay **essays** monkey **monkeys** valley **valleys**

4. For most nouns that end in *f* or *fe*, add -*s* to form the plurals.

  belief **beliefs** reef **reefs** cuff **cuffs** safe **safes**
  chief **chiefs** roof **roofs** cliff **cliffs** fife **fifes**

For some nouns that end in *f* or *fe*, change the *f* to *v* and add -*s* or -*es* to form the plurals.

  knife **knives** calf **calves** loaf **loaves**
  life **lives** leaf **leaves** thief **thieves**
  wife **wives** half **halves** shelf **shelves**

5. When a noun ends in a vowel followed by *o*, add -*s* to form the plural.

  video **videos** studio **studios** stereo **stereos**
  radio **radios** rodeo **rodeos** tattoo **tattoos**

For some nouns that end in a consonant followed by *o*, add -*es* to form the plurals.

  hero **heroes** potato **potatoes**
  echo **echoes** tomato **tomatoes**

For music words that end in a consonant followed by *o*, add -*s* to form the plurals.

  alto **altos** piano **pianos**
  solo **solos** soprano **sopranos**

6. The plurals of some words are formed in ways that cannot be explained by a rule.

  child **children** goose **geese** tooth **teeth**
  man **men** mouse **mice** foot **feet**
  woman **women** ox **oxen**

7. Sometimes the plural form of a noun is the same as its singular form. When you come across one of these nouns, the other words in the sentence should tell you whether the noun is singular or plural.

elk	**elk**	sheep	**sheep**	trout	**trout**
deer	**deer**	salmon	**salmon**	species	**species**
moose	**moose**	scissors	**scissors**	fish	**fish**

8. To form the plural of a closed compound word (a word made of two or more smaller words that has no space or hyphen between the words), add *-s* or *-es* to the last word.

spoonful	**spoonfuls**	workbench	**workbenches**
bookcase	**bookcases**	mailbox	**mailboxes**

To form the plural of an open (written as two separate words) or hyphenated (written with hyphen between the words) compound word, find the most important word and change it to its plural form.

fire engine	**fire engines**
sister-in-law	**sisters-in-law**
editor-in-chief	**editors-in-chief**

9. To form the plurals of numbers, letters, signs, and words used as words, add an apostrophe and an *s*.

> It is easier to count by **2's.**
> Charlene always forgets to dot her **I's.**
> I made the **+'s** very large and black.
> Alan has too many **and's** in that sentence.

See pages 90–91 for information on using apostrophes.

Knowing these rules can help you figure out how to form the plurals of nouns. But it is always a good idea to check a dictionary if you are not sure how to form the plural of a noun. Look for the plural form in the entry for the singular form of the word. If no plural form is shown in the entry, the plural of the word is formed simply by adding *-s*.

Possessive Nouns

The possessive form of a noun, called a **possessive noun,** is used to show who or what owns something. It can also show that the person or thing has parts.

Look at these sentences:

> The coat of Melissa is lying on a seat.
> Melissa's coat is lying on a seat.

Who does the coat belong to? It belongs to Melissa. Both sentences tell who the coat belongs to, but the first sentence sounds awkward. The second sentence sounds like something people might really say or write. *Melissa's coat* means "the coat of Melissa," "the coat that belongs to Melissa," or "the coat that Melissa owns." By adding an apostrophe and an *s* to the noun *Melissa*, the writer created the possessive form of the noun—*Melissa's*—and used it to tell who owns the coat.

> New York's subways are very crowded.

What do the subways belong to?
New York
New York's is the possessive form of *New York*.

> She stayed away from the platform's edge.

What is the edge part of?
the platform
Platform's is the possessive form of *platform*.

> The student's backpack was full of books.

Who owns the backpack?
the student
Student's is the possessive form of *student*.

22 • Nouns

How to Make Singular Nouns Possessive

Add an apostrophe and an *s* to form the possessive of a singular noun.

Singular Noun	**Possessive Form**
city	city's
noise	noise's
James	James's
train	train's

How to Make Plural Nouns Possessive

Possessives of plural nouns are formed in two ways.

1. For a plural noun that ends in *s*, add an apostrophe at the end of the word.

Plural Noun	**Possessive Form**
tunnels	tunnels'
windows	windows'
riders	riders'
lights	lights'

2. For a plural noun that does not end in s, add an apostrophe and an *s*.

Plural Noun	**Possessive Form**
people	people's
children	children's
women	women's

It is important to place the apostrophe in the correct position in a possessive noun. The meaning of the possessive changes depending on the position of the apostrophe. For example, *the girl's money* means that the money belongs to one girl. *The girls' money* means that the money belongs to two or more girls.

See pages 90–91 for information on using apostrophes.

Verbs

What Is a Verb?

A **verb** tells about an action or a state or condition.

There are two kinds of verbs: **action verbs** and **state-of-being** (or **linking**) **verbs**.

Action Verbs

An **action verb** tells about an action.

>The pitcher **threw** the ball.
>Kelly **swung** her bat.

Not all action verbs, however, tell about such physical actions, or actions that can be seen. Some action verbs tell about mental or other less obvious actions.

>Kelly **knew** how to watch a pitch.
>She **thought** about her swing.

State-of-Being or Linking Verbs

A **state-of-being verb**, which is also called a **linking verb**, tells about a state or condition. This kind of verb tells what something is, or it links the subject to words that describe or identify the subject.

The most common linking verb is the verb *be* in all its forms: *am, is, are, was, were, be, being,* and *been*. Other common linking verbs are *appear, become, feel, get, grow, look, remain, seem, smell, sound, stay,* and *taste*.

>The pitch **was** a high curve ball.
>It **seemed** higher than it really was.
>The pies **taste** good.

Some linking verbs can also be action verbs. Look at the sentence below.

>John **tastes** the pie.

Main Verbs and Helping Verbs

Look for the verbs in these sentences:

> Todd sweeps the floor.
> Janine makes the bed.

The verbs are *sweeps* and *makes*. Each verb is one word. But verbs can have more than one word.

> Todd **is sweeping** the floor.
> Janine **was making** the bed.

In these sentences, the verb is made up of two or more words. One word is the **main verb** and the other word or words are **helping verbs**.

Helping Verbs	Main Verbs
is	sweeping
was	making

Here is a list of the most common helping verbs:

be	do	can	may
being	does	could	might
been	did	will	must
am	have	would	
is	has	shall	
was	had	should	
were			

Some of these helping verbs can also be used as main verbs.

> Todd **has** the broom.
> Janine **is** in the bedroom.

The main verb and the helping verb do not have to be together in a sentence.

> Todd **did** not **sweep** the kitchen.
> **Is** Janine **putting** the sheets in the laundry basket?

Direct Objects of Verbs

A **direct object** receives the action of a verb.

With only a subject and a verb, a sentence can still express a complete thought and so be a sentence.

Claudia smiled.
Jeffrey laughed.

But often a sentence needs other words after the verb in order to express a complete thought.

Claudia took.   ?   Claudia took the book.
Jeffrey told.   ?   Jeffrey told me.

Book tells what Claudia took. Because *book* receives the action of the verb *took*, it is the direct object of the verb. *Me* tells whom Jeffrey told. Because *me* receives the action of the verb *told*, it is the direct object of the verb.

For a word to receive the action of a verb, the verb must have an action to send. It must be an action verb. A linking verb, which does not express an action, cannot have a direct object.

To identify the direct object in a sentence, find the verb and ask *whom* or *what*. The answer to the question is the direct object.

Jeffrey invited Claudia to a party.
Jeffrey invited whom? Claudia
Claudia is the direct object.

Claudia bought a gift for Jeffrey.
Claudia bought what? gift
Gift is the direct object.

Words After Linking Verbs

An action verb can be followed by a word in the predicate that receives the action of the verb. This word is called a direct object. Only an action verb can have a direct object. A state-of-being or linking verb cannot have a direct object. However, a linking verb can be followed by a word in the predicate that describes or tells about the subject of the sentence. This word is called a **predicate word.**

> The soup is **hot.**
> The bread is **fresh.**

In each sentence, a linking verb *(is)* links or connects the subject with a predicate word that describes or tells about the subject. The word *hot* describes the subject *soup*. The word *fresh* describes the subject *bread*.

A predicate word can be an adjective, a noun, or a pronoun.

> The baked chicken tastes spicy.
> *Spicy* describes the subject *chicken*.
> *Spicy* is an adjective.

> The green bean casserole is a new dish.
> *Dish* tells about the subject *casserole*.
> *Dish* is a noun.

> The most creative chef is she.
> *She* tells about the subject *chef*.
> *She* is a pronoun.

Only linking verbs can be followed by predicate words that tell about the subject. Remember, linking verbs are words such as *am, is, are, was, were, be, being, been, appear, become, feel, get, grow, look, remain, seem, smell, sound, stay,* and *taste.*

Subject-Verb Agreement

Remember, a singular noun names one person, place, thing, or idea.

       cat   girl   book

A plural noun names more than one person, place, thing, or idea.

       cats   girls   books

Just as nouns can be singular or plural, verbs can be singular or plural. Verbs must agree in number with the subjects in their sentences. "Agree in number" means that if the subject is singular, the verb must be singular, and if the subject is plural, the verb must be plural.

A **cat jumps** down.	The **cats jump** down.
The **girl plays** a game.	The **girls play** a game.
A **book falls** over.	Three **books fall** over.

In the example sentences on the left, the subjects *cat*, *girl*, and *book* are singular. The verbs *jumps*, *plays*, and *falls* are singular. The singular verbs agree in number with the singular nouns *cat*, *girl*, and *book*.

In the example sentences on the right, the subjects *cats*, *girls*, and *books* are plural. The verbs *jump*, *play*, and *fall* are plural. The plural verbs agree in number with the plural nouns *cats*, *girls*, and *books*.

You can find out more about the different forms of verbs on pages 29–33.

A few verbs and other words have special singular and plural forms that you need to remember. (See exceptions on page 46.)

Be, Do, Have

Some of the forms of the verb *be* are *is*, *are*, *was*, and *were*. The forms *is* and *was* are singular. The forms *are* and *were* are plural.

> The book **is** mine.   The book **was** mine.
> The cats **are** playing.   The cats **were** playing.

Two forms of the verb *do* are *does* and *do*. The form *does* is singular. The form *do* is plural.

> The girl **does** want that book.
> The girls **do** want that book.

Two forms of the verb *have* are *has* and *have*. The form *has* is singular. The form *have* is plural.

> The girl **has** a cat.
> The girls **have** a cat.

Here, There, Where

Some sentences begin with the words *here*, *there*, and *where*.

> Here are the cats.
> There is the girl.
> Where are the books?

Here, *there*, and *where* are not the subjects of the sentences. Find the subject by finding the verb and asking *who* or *what*. For example, who or what are here? The cats are. The word *cats* is the subject of the first sentence. Because the word *cats* is plural, the plural verb *are* is used in the sentence. Look at the second sentence. Who or what is there? The girl is. The girl is the subject of the sentence. The verb must agree in number with the subject.

Verbs • 29

Verb Tenses

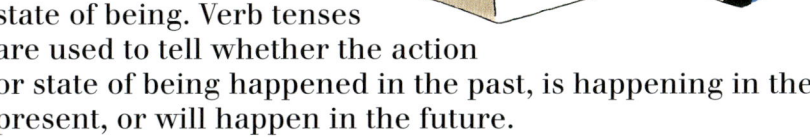

Verbs have different forms, which are called **tenses**. These tenses are used to show time. Remember, verbs tell about an action or a state of being. Verb tenses are used to tell whether the action or state of being happened in the past, is happening in the present, or will happen in the future.

Present	I **am** a writer.	I **work** at home.
Past	I **was** there all day.	I **wrote** an article.
Future	I **will be** there tomorrow.	I **will call** you.

Present Tense

The **present tense** tells about an action or a state of being that is happening now.

To form the present tense:

• with a singular subject, add *-s* or *-es* to the base form of the verb—the form with no endings.

>George **repairs** cars.   He **fixes** the engines.

• with a plural subject, use the base form of the verb.

>The Goldmans **own** a restaurant.   They **serve** pizza.

• with the pronouns *I* and *you,* use the base form of the verb.

>I **manage** a store.
>You **design** houses.

Past Tense

The **past tense** tells about an action or a state of being that happened in the past.

30 • Verbs

To form the past tense of most verbs:

• add *-ed* or *-d* to the base form of the verb. Verbs that form the past tense in this way are called **regular verbs**.

repair	repaired	fix	fixed
own	owned	serve	served
manage	managed	design	designed

To form the past tense of other verbs:

• change the spelling of the verb. Verbs that form the past tense in this way are called **irregular verbs**. The spellings of the past tense forms of irregular verbs have to be memorized.

write	wrote	build	built
draw	drew	teach	taught
sell	sold	make	made

Future Tense

The **future tense** tells about an action or a state of being that will happen in the future.

To form the future tense of verbs:

• use the helping verbs *will* or *shall* with the base form of the verb.

    paint   will paint   cook will cook

Using More than One Verb

When using verb tenses, the important thing to remember is to keep all the verbs in the same tense. For example, if one verb is in the present tense, then the other verb or verbs should be in the present tense, whether they are in the same sentence or different sentences.

Nina **typed, edited,** and **filed** medical reports.
(All three verbs are in the past tense.)

Ed **drives** a truck. He **makes** deliveries to stores.
(Both verbs are in the present tense.)

Parts of Verbs

Every verb has several different forms. Every verb also has three **parts:** present, past, and past participle. A verb's forms are made from these three parts.

Here are some examples of verbs and their parts:

Present	Past	Past Participle
work	worked	(have) worked
wash	washed	(have) washed
clean	cleaned	(have) cleaned
wrap	wrapped	(have) wrapped
dry	dried	(have) dried

The present part of a verb is the same as its present tense form. The future tense is formed using the present part and the helping verb *will* or *shall*.

The past part of a verb is the same as its past tense form. For most verbs, the past form is made by adding *-ed* to the present form. But if the present form of a verb ends in *y* or has a short vowel sound and a single final consonant, the spelling of its past form changes (study, studied).

The past participle part of a verb is not the same as any one tense form. The past participle is used with helping verbs to form three additional verb tenses: present perfect, past perfect, and future perfect.

Present Perfect	has dusted	have scrubbed
Past Perfect	had dusted	had scrubbed
Future Perfect	will have dusted	will have scrubbed

All the examples on this page are regular verbs. Their past forms are made by adding *-ed* to their present forms, and their past forms are the same as their past participle forms. See pages 32–33 for information on the past and past participle forms of irregular verbs.

Irregular Verbs

Remember, regular verbs are verbs whose past forms are made by adding *-ed* to their present forms.

| laugh | **laughed** | dance | **danced** |
| smile | **smiled** | walk | **walked** |

Irregular verbs are verbs whose past forms are spelled differently from their present forms.

| come | **came** | eat | **ate** |
| fly | **flew** | see | **saw** |

With regular verbs, the past participle is the same as the past form.

| play | **played** | (have) **played** |
| talk | **talked** | (have) **talked** |

For some irregular verbs, the past participle is also the same as the past form.

| bring | **brought** | (have) **brought** |
| hear | **heard** | (have) **heard** |

But for many irregular verbs, the past participle is not the same as the past form.

| sing | **sang** | (have) **sung** |
| write | **wrote** | (have) **written** |

With both regular and irregular verbs, the past form is always used *without* a helping verb.

> Elena **grew** tomatoes and peppers in her garden.

With both regular and irregular verbs, the past participle is always used *with* a helping verb.

> Elena **has grown** tomatoes and peppers in her garden every year.

The following page lists the parts of many common irregular verbs. Use the list to check the forms of the verbs you write. Remember, a dictionary gives the parts of an irregular verb in the entry for the present form.

Parts of Irregular Verbs

Present	Past	Past Participle
begin	began	(have) begun
bring	brought	(have) brought
build	built	(have) built
choose	chose	(have) chosen
come	came	(have) come
do	did	(have) done
draw	drew	(have) drawn
drink	drank	(have) drunk
drive	drove	(have) driven
eat	ate	(have) eaten
fall	fell	(have) fallen
fly	flew	(have) flown
freeze	froze	(have) frozen
give	gave	(have) given
go	went	(have) gone
grow	grew	(have) grown
hear	heard	(have) heard
hide	hid	(have) hidden
keep	kept	(have) kept
know	knew	(have) known
make	made	(have) made
read	read	(have) read
ride	rode	(have) ridden
run	ran	(have) run
say	said	(have) said
see	saw	(have) seen
sell	sold	(have) sold
sing	sang	(have) sung
sit	sat	(have) sat
speak	spoke	(have) spoken
swim	swam	(have) swum
take	took	(have) taken
teach	taught	(have) taught
think	thought	(have) thought
throw	threw	(have) thrown
wear	wore	(have) worn
write	wrote	(have) written

Confusing Verbs

Writers often confuse these pairs of verbs. Learning the meanings of the verbs can help you use them correctly.

Bring–Take

Bring means "to come with or carry something from another place." *Take* means "to grasp" or "to carry away."

> bring, brought,   take, took,
> (have) brought   (have) taken

> Will you **bring** that plate to me?
> Please **take** a sandwich to Aunt Gertrude.

Can–May

Can means "to be able to." *May* means "to be allowed or permitted to."

> can, could   may, might

> Deborah **can** wiggle her ears.
> **May** I go swimming now?

Lead–Led

The noun *lead* (pronounced with a short *e* sound) is the name of a metal often used to make pipes. *Lead* (pronounced with a long *e* sound) is a verb that means "to show the way." *Led* is the past tense form of the verb *lead*.

> lead, led, (have) led

> This basket is as heavy as **lead.**
> Who will **lead** us to the picnic area?
> Jack **led** the children through the woods.

Let–Leave

Let means "to allow or permit." *Leave* means "to go away" or "to let stay as is."

> let, let, (have) let   leave, left, (have) left

> Molly **let** Karen choose a prize first.
> Michael won't **leave** until you do.
> Don't **leave** any food or trash behind.

Lie–Lay

Lie means "to rest" or "to be in a horizontal position." *Lie* cannot take a direct object. *Lay* means "to place or put down." *Lay* can take a direct object.

>lie, lay, (have) lain   lay, laid, (have) laid
>
>Will you **lie** down in the shade and take a nap?
>You can **lay** the newspaper over your face.

Rise–Raise

Rise means "to go upward." *Rise* cannot take a direct object. *Raise* means "to cause to go up." *Raise* can take a direct object. When the subject of the sentence is moving upward, use *rise*. When the subject of the sentence is making something else move upward, use *raise*.

>rise, rose,   raise, raised,
>(have) risen   (have) raised
>
>The kite **rises** high above the trees.
>David **raises** the kite high over his head.

Sit means "to occupy a seat." *Sit* cannot take a direct object. *Set* means "to put or place." *Set* can take a direct object.

>sit, sat, (have) sat   set, set, (have) set
>
>We **sat** on the grass to eat.
>Who **set** their dirty shoes on the blanket?

Teach–Learn

Teach means "to instruct or help to learn." *Learn* means "to gain knowledge."

>teach, taught,   learn, learned,
>(have) taught   (have) learned
>
>Allison **taught** the children how to play badminton.
>They **learned** the game very quickly.

Pronouns

What Is a Pronoun?

A **pronoun** is a word used to replace a noun. The noun that the pronoun replaces is called the **antecedent**.

Remember, nouns name people, places, things, or ideas. Pronouns can also be used to refer to these people, places, things, or ideas.

> Celia tried to catch Celia's cat so Celia could take the cat to the vet.

> Celia tried to catch her cat so she could take it to the vet.

Repeating the nouns in the first sentence makes the sentence very awkward. Replacing some of the nouns with pronouns makes the second sentence less awkward. *Her, she,* and *it* are pronouns. *Her* and *she* replace *Celia's* and *Celia. It* replaces *the cat.* The word or words a pronoun replaces are the antecedent of the pronoun. *Celia's* is the antecedent of *her. Celia* is the antecedent of *she. The cat* is the antecedent of *it.*

Sometimes the antecedent of a pronoun is another pronoun.

> Did Celia help you when your cat was sick?
> (*You* is the antecedent of *your.*)

Sometimes two or more nouns may be the antecedent of a pronoun.

> Celia and David take good care of their pets.
> (*Celia* and *David* are the antecedents of *their.*)

Sometimes the antecedent may be understood. It is not a word in the sentence, but the writer and reader understand who the antecedent is. In such cases, the antecedent is usually the person speaking.

> Bunky, a dachshund, is **my** favorite.
> (The antecedent of *my* is the speaker.)

Usually, a pronoun appears after the antecedent in the same sentence. But sometimes the pronoun appears in one sentence, and the antecedent appears in another sentence.

> The **kitten** is very playful. **It** chases **its** tail.
> (*Kitten* is the antecedent of *It* and *its*.)

Pronouns can be singular or plural. They can be used to refer to the speaker, to the person spoken to, or to the person, place, thing, or idea spoken about. (For more information on these ideas, see page 38.)

Singular Pronouns

Speaker	I	me	my, mine
Person spoken to	you	you	your, yours
People, places, things spoken about	he she it	him her it	his her, hers its

Plural Pronouns

Speaker	we	us	our, ours
Person spoken to	you	you	your, yours
People, places, things spoken about	they	them	their, theirs

Just as verbs must agree in number with the subjects of their sentences, pronouns must agree in number with their antecedents. When an antecedent is singular, use a singular pronoun. When an antecedent is plural, use a plural pronoun.

> The **cat** hid under the bed. **It** refused to come out.
> The **dogs** barked noisily. **They** heard something.

Personal Pronouns

The chart on page 37 lists personal pronouns according to their number (singular or plural) and their person. There are three persons: first, second, and third. **First person** is the person speaking, or the speaker. **Second person** is the person spoken to. **Third person** is the person, place, or thing spoken about.

First Person
I called.

Second Person
You called.

Third Person
They called.

Personal pronouns can also be grouped according to their **case.** There are three cases: nominative, objective, and possessive. A pronoun used as a subject in a sentence is in the **nominative** case. A pronoun used as an object is in the **objective** case. A pronoun that shows ownership is in the **possessive** case.

Nominative
I saw Ann.

Objective
Ann saw **me**.

Possessive
Ann is **my** friend.

Singular Pronouns

	Nominative	Objective	Possessive
First person	I	me	my, mine
Second person	you	you	your, yours
Third person	he	him	his
	she	her	her, hers
	it	it	its

Plural Pronouns

	Nominative	Objective	Possessive
First person	we	us	our, ours
Second person	you	you	your, yours
Third person	they	them	their, theirs

Personal pronouns change forms. They change forms to show number; to show first, second, or third person; and to show their use in a sentence.

Using Pronouns as Subjects and Objects

Pronouns as Subjects

The subject pronouns are *I, you, he, she, it, we,* and *they.* When pronouns appear as the subjects of sentences or after linking verbs, these forms are used.

Only subject pronouns can be used as the subject of a verb.

> After school Gerald went to his flute lesson.
> **He** has been taking lessons for a year.
>
> Janet hurried to soccer practice.
> **She** did not want to be late again.

Gerald is the subject of the first sentence. *He* is the subject of the second sentence. The form *he* is used because it is a subject pronoun. *Janet* is the subject of the third sentence. *She* is the subject of the fourth sentence. The form *she* is used because it is a subject pronoun. Pronouns such as *him* and *her* could not be used as the subjects because they are not subject pronouns.

Sometimes a pronoun appears as part of a compound subject.

> Janet and **he** made the team.
> Gerald and **she** will play a duet.

Because the pronouns in the sentences are part of compound subjects, the subject pronouns *he* and *she* are used.

To decide what pronoun should be used, put each part of the compound subject in its own sentence.

> **Janet** made the team. **He** made the team.
> **Gerald** will play a duet. **She** will play a duet.

Then combine the subjects, keeping the same pronoun used when the sentences were separate.

Sometimes a compound subject is joined by *or* or *nor*.

>Either **Janet** or **I** will be the goalie.
>Neither **Gerald** nor **she** can practice today.

To decide what pronoun should be used, use the same steps as with a compound subject joined by *and*. Leave out words such as *or, nor, neither,* or *either*.

>**Janet** will be the goalie. **I** will be the goalie.
>**Gerald** can practice today. **She** can practice today.

Then combine the subjects, keeping the same pronouns and putting back in the conjunctions.

Sometimes a pronoun is followed by a noun in the subject of a sentence. To decide what pronoun to use in the sentence, read the sentence, leaving out the noun.

>**We** soccer players are not afraid of hard work.
>**We** are not afraid of hard work.

>**We** flute players know all about hard work, too.
>**We** know all about hard work, too.

Subject pronouns are also used after linking verbs.

>**She** is an athlete.   An athlete is **she**.
>**He** is an artist.   An artist is **he**.

In the sentences on the left, *she* and *he* are the subjects. Therefore, subject pronouns were used. In the sentences on the right, the pronouns follow the linking verb *is* and identify the subjects *athlete* and *artist*. Therefore, the subject pronouns *she* and *he* were used.

Pronouns as Objects

The object pronouns are *me, you, him, her, it, us,* and *them*. When pronouns appear as the objects of verbs or prepositions in sentences, these are the forms that are used.

Unlike nouns, when pronouns are used as the objects of action verbs, they change their forms. *You* and *it* are used as both subject and object pronouns, but the other object pronouns are different from their subject forms.

Subject	Object
I	me
he	him
she	her
we	us
they	them

Only object pronouns can be used as the object of a verb.

    Janet told Alice to kick.   Janet told **her** to kick.
    Gerald gave the music to Joe.   Gerald gave **it** to Joe.

Sometimes a pronoun appears as part of a compound object.

    The teacher asked Gerald and **him** to play.

To decide what pronoun should be used, put each part of the compound object in its own sentence. Then combine the objects, keeping the same pronoun used when the sentences were separate.

    The teacher asked **Gerald** to play.
    The teacher asked **him** to play.

Object pronouns are also used as objects of prepositions. A preposition is a word that relates a noun or a pronoun to another word in the sentence. The noun or pronoun that follows the preposition is called the object of the preposition.

    The coach gave advice to Janet.
    The coach gave advice to **her.**

See pages 60–65 for information on prepositions.

Possessive Pronouns

Like possessive nouns, **possessive pronouns** show ownership. The possessive pronouns are *my, mine, your, yours, his, her, hers, its, our, ours, their,* and *theirs.*

    Your coat is the same color as **her** jacket.
    His new shoes came from **my** shop.

The pronoun *your* tells to whom the coat belongs. The pronoun *her* tells who the jacket belongs to. The pronouns *his* and *my* tell who owns the shoes and the shop.

Unlike nouns, pronouns do not form their possessives by adding an apostrophe and an *s*. Pronouns change their forms to show the possessive case. These forms never use apostrophes.

The possessive pronouns *mine, yours, hers, ours,* and *theirs* are used alone. *His* and *its* can be used alone or as adjectives. An **adjective** modifies, or describes, a noun or a pronoun. The possessive pronouns *my, your, her, our,* and *their* are used as adjectives.

    The hat is **mine.**   This is **my** hat.

(*Mine* tells to whom the hat belongs. It is used as a predicate word. *My* also tells whom the hat belongs to. It is used as an adjective. It modifies *hat.*)

Do not confuse possessive pronouns with contractions that sound similar but are spelled differently and, of course, mean different things.

    Is this **your** glove?   (possessive pronoun)
    You're missing one.   (contraction for *You are*)

    The scarf has lost **its** fringe.   (possessive pronoun)
    It's a very old scarf.   (contraction for *It is*)

    I see **their** caps.   (possessive pronoun)
    They're in that box.   (contraction for *They are*)

Indefinite Pronouns

Some pronouns do not refer to any specific person or thing. These pronouns are called **indefinite pronouns.** Because they do not refer to any specific person or thing, indefinite pronouns often do not have antecedents in their sentences. Sometimes their antecedents are people or things understood by the reader. Sometimes their antecedents are simply unknown.

Everybody enjoyed the art exhibit.
(*Everybody* has no antecedent.)

Many of the paintings came from other museums.
(*Many* refers to paintings.)

Here is a list of indefinite pronouns:

Indefinite Pronouns

Singular
one	anybody	something	other
anyone	somebody	nothing	another
someone	nobody	everything	one another
everyone	everybody	each	either
no one	anything	each other	neither

Plural
many	few	several	others	both

Singular or Plural
all	some	any	most	none

When using indefinite pronouns,

- use *his, her,* and *its* with singular pronouns.

  One of the men lost **his** ticket.
  Each of the women had **her** own tape recorder.

- use *his or her* if the person could be either male or female.

  Everyone moved at **his or her** own pace.

- use *their* with plural pronouns.

  Neither lost **their** seats.

Demonstrative, Relative, and Interrogative Pronouns

Demonstrative Pronouns

Demonstrative pronouns are used to point out persons and things. The demonstrative pronouns are *this, that, these,* and *those. This* and *that* are singular pronouns. *These* and *those* are plural pronouns.

This is my sister.
That is my sister.

These are my sisters.
Those are my sisters.

This and *these* point out people or things that are close in space or time. *That* and *those* point out people or things that are farther away.

This is my brother.

That is my brother.

Relative Pronouns

A **relative pronoun** is used to introduce an adjective clause in a sentence. It connects the clause to the noun or pronoun the clause modifies. A clause is a group of words that has a subject and a verb but cannot stand alone as a sentence. The relative pronouns are *who, whom, whose, that, which,* and *what.*

Who, whom, and *whose* are used to refer to people. *That* is used to refer to things or people. *Which* and *what* are used to refer to things.

> The man **who** waved to us is my uncle.
> The cousin to **whom** I wrote a letter wrote back.
> The student **whose** essay won the contest is my sister.
> Dad read the book **that** was on the best-seller list.
> Aunt Joyce is the woman **that** brought the flowers.
> Mom likes green, **which** is also Dad's favorite color.
> A family dinner is **what** I'm looking forward to.

The noun or pronoun that the adjective clause modifies is the antecedent of the relative pronoun. For example, in the first sentence, the antecedent of the relative pronoun *who* is the noun *man.* In the second sentence, the antecedent of the relative pronoun *whom* is the noun *cousin.*

Interrogative Pronouns

Interrogative pronouns introduce questions. The interrogative pronouns are *who, whom, whose, which,* and *what. Who, whom,* and *whose* are used to refer to people. *What* is used to refer to things, places, or ideas. *Which* can be used to refer to people or things. Use *which* if the answer is a choice between two or more things.

> **Who** wants some of Uncle Paul's mashed potatoes?
> **What** is Aunt Stella bringing to the dinner?
> **Which** did you try—the green beans or the carrots?

An interrogative pronoun does not have an antecedent.

Subject-Verb Agreement

Indefinite pronouns and the pronouns *you* and *I* have special rules of agreement that you need to remember.

Indefinite Pronouns

Some indefinite pronouns are singular. They always use singular verbs. Some indefinite pronouns are plural. They always use plural verbs.

> **Everybody likes** to travel light. (singular)
> **Neither** of my bags **is** very heavy. (singular)
> **Both are** made of lightweight nylon. (plural)

Some indefinite pronouns can be singular or plural, depending on whether they are referring to one thing or several things.

> **All** of my money **is** in my tote bag. (one thing)
> **All** of my clothes **are** in my suitcase. (several things)

See page 43 for a complete list of singular, plural, and singular/plural indefinite pronouns.

You–I

Even though the pronoun *I* is always a singular subject, it uses plural forms of verbs. The only exceptions are the verbs *am* and *was*, which are singular verb forms.

> I **am** ready to go.   I **was** packed hours ago.
> I **travel** alone.   I **see** things.   I **meet** people.

Even though the pronoun *you* can be either singular or plural, it always uses plural forms of verbs.

> I said to the guide, "You **were** very helpful."
> I said to my fellow travelers, "You **were** very helpful, too."

Chapter 5 • 47

Adjectives

What Is an Adjective?

An **adjective** is a word that tells about a noun or a pronoun.

Look for the nouns in these sentences.

> The children hike along the trail.
> The noisy children hike along the hot, dry trail.

Which sentence tells more about the children and the trail? In the second sentence, the word *noisy* tells about the noun *children,* and the words *hot* and *dry* describe the noun *trail.* Words such as *noisy, hot,* and *dry* that describe, or modify, nouns or pronouns are called adjectives.

Sometimes two or more adjectives modify the same word. You may have to separate the adjectives with commas.

> The **small, brown** lizard scurries under a rock.
> The lizard looks for a **cool, dark, hidden** hole.

Adjectives are usually placed before the word they modify. However, they may also be placed after the word they modify.

> The **tall, majestic** cactus stands alone.
> The cactus, **tall** and **majestic,** stands alone.

How Adjectives Modify

An adjective modifies a word by answering one of these questions about the word: What kind? How many? Which one?

48 • Adjectives

- The adjectives in this sentence tell *what kind*.

    The **weary** hikers took off their **heavy** backpacks by the **cool** stream.
    (What kind of hikers? Weary ones. What kind of backpacks? Heavy ones. What kind of stream? A cool one.)

- The adjectives in this sentence tell *how many*.

    The hikers saw **six** snakes, **many** spiders, and **several** coyotes.
    (How many snakes? Six. How many spiders? Many. How many coyotes? Several.)

- The adjectives in this sentence tell *which one*.

    That hiker is making **her third** trip on **this** trail.
    (Which hiker? That one. Which trip? Her trip. Third trip. Which trail? This one.)

Remember, possessive pronouns are used as adjectives. They tell *which one* or *which ones*.

Proper Adjectives

Adjectives that are made by adding endings to proper nouns are called *proper adjectives*. Like proper nouns, proper adjectives are always capitalized. Like common nouns, common adjectives are not capitalized.

Proper Noun	**Proper Adjective**
New Mexico	New Mexican
America	American

Common Noun	**Common Adjective**
rock	rocky
beauty	beautiful

When a proper noun is used as an adjective, it is still capitalized.

The trail led from the **Utah** border into the **Arizona** desert.

See page 17 for information on common and proper nouns and pages 72–75 for information on capitalizing proper nouns and adjectives.

Articles, Demonstrative Adjectives, Possessive Adjectives

Articles

The words *a, an,* and *the* are called **articles.** Articles always modify nouns. Therefore, articles are adjectives.

• *The* is used to refer to a particular person, place, thing, or idea. *A* and *an* are used to refer to one of a general group of people, places, things, or ideas.

> He caught **the** beetle. (a particular beetle)
> He caught **a** beetle. (any beetle)

• *A* and *an* are used with singular nouns. *The* can be used with either singular or plural nouns.

> **a** cricket   **the** ladybug
> **an** ant   **the** caterpillars

• Use *a* with words that begin with a consonant sound. Use *an* with words that begin with a vowel sound.

> **a** mosquito   **a** large moth
> **an** insect   **an** unusual fly

• Use *an* with words that begin with a silent *h.*

> **an** hour   **an** honor   **an** honest effort

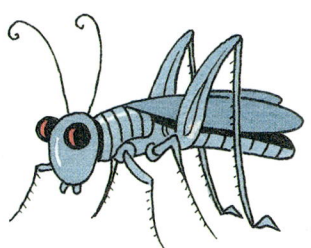

Demonstrative Adjectives

This, that, these, and *those* are **demonstrative adjectives.** They are used to point out people and things. *This* and *these* are used to point out people or things that are close in space or time. *That* and *those* are used to point out people or things that are farther away. *This* and *that* are used with singular nouns. *These* and *those* are used with plural nouns.

> **This** butterfly is yellow.   **That** butterfly is orange.
> **These** ants eat leaves.   **Those** ants eat seeds.

On page 44, *this, that, these,* and *those* were described as demonstrative pronouns. These words can function as either pronouns or adjectives. They are pronouns when they take the place of nouns. They are adjectives when they modify nouns by answering the question "Which one?"

> **This** wasp is buzzing around my head. (adjective)
> **This** is a problem! (pronoun)

> **Those** wasps won't sting you. (adjective)
> **Those** are not the stinging kind. (pronoun)

Possessive Adjectives

Possessive nouns were discussed as nouns on pages 21–22, and possessive pronouns were discussed as pronouns on page 42. Both possessive nouns and possessive pronouns function as adjectives when they are used to modify nouns and pronouns in sentences. All possessive nouns can be used as adjectives. Only the possessive pronouns *my, your, his, her, its, our,* and *their* can be used as adjectives.

> **Alan's** dream is to be an entomologist like **his** father. (Possessive noun *Alan's* modifies noun *dream;* possessive pronoun *his* modifies noun *father.*)

> **Their** study is about the **insects'** feeding habits. (Possessive pronoun *their* modifies noun *study;* possessive noun *insects'* modifies noun *habits.*)

Predicate Adjectives

A **predicate adjective** is an adjective that follows a linking verb and modifies the subject of the sentence.

Some adjectives follow a linking verb. Because these adjectives appear in the predicate of the sentence, they are called *predicate adjectives*.

predicate

The animals seemed very **restless** today.

A predicate adjective describes the subject of the sentence. In the example sentence, the predicate adjective *restless* follows the linking verb *seemed* and modifies the subject *animals*.

One predicate adjective can modify a compound subject. Two predicate adjectives can modify a single subject.

The **chickens** and the **horses** were **nervous.**
(*Nervous* modifies *chickens* and *horses*.)

But the **cows** remained **calm** and **indifferent.**
(*Calm* and *indifferent* modify *cows*.)

Note that a predicate adjective comes after the word it modifies. (Most adjectives come before the words they modify.) The predicate adjective is separated from the subject by the linking verb and often by other words as well.

Remember, linking verbs are verbs that express a state or condition, not an action. Here are some common linking verbs:

am	was	become	remain	sound
is	were	feel	seem	stay
are	appear	look	smell	taste

See page 23 for information on linking verbs. See page 26 for information on words that come after linking verbs.

52 • Adjectives

Comparing with Adjectives

Adjectives have two special forms that are used to compare things. The **comparative form** of an adjective is used when two things are compared. The **superlative form** of the adjective is used when three or more things are compared.

>The dog is big. The elephant is big. The whale is big.

All three animals may be big, but some are bigger than others. To compare the bigness of the animals, use the comparative and superlative forms of the adjective *big*.

Use the comparative form *bigger* to compare two of the animals.

>The elephant is **bigger** than the dog.
>The whale is **bigger** than the elephant.

Use the superlative form *biggest* to compare all three of the animals.

>The whale is the **biggest** of all three animals.

Endings *-er* and *-est*

- Add *-er* to make the comparative form of most short adjectives.

- Add *-est* to make the superlative form of most short adjectives.

Adjective	Comparative	Superlative
large	larger	largest
small	smaller	smallest
wet	wetter	wettest
fast	faster	fastest
dry	drier	driest
slow	slower	slowest

Notice the spelling changes that must take place in some adjectives before -er or -est is added. For an adjective that ends in e, such as *large*, drop the e before adding -er or -est. For an adjective ending in a short vowel and a single consonant, such as *wet*, double the final consonant before adding -er or -est. For an adjective that ends in a consonant and a *y*, such as *dry*, change the *y* to an *i* before adding -er or -est.

More and Most

- To make the comparative form of an adjective with two or more syllables, use the word *more* with the adjective.

- To make the superlative form of an adjective with two or more syllables, use the word *most* with the adjective.

Adjective	Comparative	Superlative
graceful	more graceful	most graceful
active	more active	most active
dangerous	more dangerous	most dangerous
intelligent	more intelligent	most intelligent

Irregular Forms

Some adjectives have comparative and superlative forms that are formed differently.

Adjective	Comparative	Superlative
good	better	best
bad	worse	worst
far	farther	farthest
many	more	most

See pages 57–58 for information on comparing with adverbs.

Adverbs

What Is an Adverb?

An **adverb** is a word that modifies a verb, an adjective, or another adverb.

Remember, an adjective modifies a noun or a pronoun. That is, it tells something about the noun or pronoun. An adverb modifies a verb, an adjective, or another adverb. It tells about the verb, adjective, or adverb.

> The carpenter looks **closely** at the wood.
> (*Closely* modifies the verb *looks*.)
> The old cabinet is **truly** beautiful.
> (*Truly* modifies the adjective *beautiful*.)
> She begins to clean it **very** carefully.
> (*Very* modifies the adverb *carefully*.)

Adjectives tell *what kind, how many*, and *which one* about the words they modify. Adverbs tell *how, when, where*, and *how much* about the words they modify.

> Sara works **patiently.**   (Works *how?* Patiently.)
> She will be finished **soon.** (Finished *when?* Soon.)
> The cabinet stands **there.**   (Stands *where?* There.)

Adverbs that modify adjectives and adverbs usually come before the words they modify. Adverbs that modify verbs usually come after the verb, but they can be found in other locations in the sentence.

> **Now** the wood is old.   The wood **now** is old.
> The wood is old **now.**

Many adverbs are easy to identify because they have the ending *-ly*.

> slowly   finally   promptly   exactly

However, many adverbs do not have the *-ly* ending.

> almost   never   often   yesterday

Adjectives and Adverbs

Look at these two sets of words:

loud	loudly
slow	slowly
bright	brightly
sudden	suddenly
happy	happily
pleasant	pleasantly
beautiful	beautifully
furious	furiously

The two sets don't look very different from each other, do they? All the words are modifiers. The main difference between the adjectives on the left and the adverbs on the right is the words they modify.

Remember:

• **Adjectives** modify nouns and pronouns.
They tell *what kind*, *how many*, or *which one* about the nouns and pronouns they modify.

• **Adverbs** modify verbs, adjectives, and other adverbs. They tell *how*, *when*, *where*, or *how much* about the verbs, adjectives, and other adverbs they modify.

How do you decide whether to use an adjective or an adverb in a sentence? Ask this question: "What word is being modified?"

The sun shone _____ in the sky.
            bright, brightly

To choose between the adjective *bright* and the adverb *brightly*, ask what word in the sentence is being modified. The verb *shone* is being modified. Only adverbs can modify verbs, so the adverb *brightly* is the correct word.

56 • Adverbs

After the shower, the flowers looked _____.
beautiful, beautifully

To choose between the adjective *beautiful* and the adverb *beautifully,* ask what word in the sentence is being modified. Notice that *looked* is used as a linking verb. A linking verb links the subject to words in the predicate that describe the subject. So the word being modified is the noun *flowers.* Only adjectives can modify nouns, so the adjective *beautiful* is the correct word.

Good–Well and *Bad–Badly*

In the pairs of words *good/well* and *bad/badly,* which are the adjectives and which are the adverbs? Writers and speakers often confuse these words.

- *Good* and *bad* are adjectives.

    > The wet grass smells **good.**
    > (*Smells* is used as a linking verb.
    > *Good* is a predicate adjective.)

    > Don't feel **bad** about the mud.
    > (*Feel* is used as a linking verb.
    > *Bad* is a predicate adjective.)

- *Well* and *badly* are adverbs.

    > My new umbrella worked **well** during the rain.
    > (How did it work? Well.)

    > I **badly** needed a new umbrella.
    > (How did I need? Badly.)

- When *well* is used to mean "healthy" and to describe a noun or pronoun, it is an adjective. In the sentence "I feel *well,*" *well* is an adjective.

Comparing with Adverbs

Like adjectives, adverbs have two special forms that are used to make comparisons. The **comparative form** of an adverb is used when two actions are compared. The **superlative form** of the adverb is used when three or more actions are compared.

> Sam runs fast. Leon runs fast. Jose runs fast.

All three boys run fast, but they do not all run at the same speed. To compare the actions of the runners, use the comparative and superlative forms of the adverb *fast*.

Use the comparative form *faster* to compare the actions of two of the runners.

> Leon runs **faster** than Sam.
> Jose runs **faster** than Leon.

Use the superlative form *fastest* to compare the actions of all three runners.

> Of the three, Jose runs the **fastest.**

Endings *-er* and *-est*

• Add *-er* to make the comparative form of some short adverbs.

• Add *-est* to make the superlative form of some short adverbs.

Adverb	Comparative	Superlative
hard	harder	hardest
late	later	latest
soon	sooner	soonest
early	earlier	earliest

More and *Most*

- To make the comparative form of an adverb that ends in *-ly*, use the word *more* with the adverb.

- To make the superlative form of an adverb that ends in *-ly*, use the word *most* with the adverb.

Adverb	Comparative	Superlative
quietly	more quietly	most quietly
rapidly	more rapidly	most rapidly
happily	more happily	most happily
fearfully	more fearfully	most fearfully

Irregular Forms

Some adverbs have comparative and superlative forms that have nothing to do with adding either endings or words.

Adverb	Comparative	Superlative
well	better	best
badly	worse	worst
little	less	least
much	more	most

Many adverbs cannot be used to make comparisons. These adverbs do not have comparative and superlative forms. Often these adverbs answer the questions "Where?" and "When?" Examples include *here, there, inside, outside, everywhere, yesterday, today, tomorrow,* and *now.*

In autumn, we play **outside.** (*Where* do we play? outside)

Leaves are falling **everywhere.** (*Where* are leaves falling? everywhere)

Today, we'll play in Trini's yard (*When* will we play? today)

- When comparing the action of one person or thing to the actions of a group the person or thing belongs to, use the comparative form of the adverb and include the word *other* or *else.*

Jose runs **faster** than any **other** boy.
Jose runs **faster** than anyone **else** in the school.

See pages 52–53 for information on comparing with adjectives.

Double Negatives

Two negatives in the same sentence is one negative too many.

A negative is a word that means "no." Of course, the word *no* means "no." So do some words that have *no* in them.

nobody   no one   nothing
none   nowhere   not

But some negatives do not have *no* in them.

never   hardly   barely   scarcely

The negative word *not* is used in many contractions. In a contraction, *not* is spelled *-n't* and is combined with another word. This can make the *not* harder to see. Because *not* means "no," contractions with *-n't* are also negatives.

is + *not* = isn't
has + *not* = hasn't
are + *not* = aren't
can + *not* = can't
was + *not* = wasn't
could + *not* = couldn't
were + *not* = weren't
will + *not* = won't
do + *not* = don't
would + *not* = wouldn't
did + *not* = didn't
should + *not* = shouldn't
have + *not* = haven't

Two negatives in the same sentence is called a **double negative.** A sentence does not need more than one negative.

Incorrect   I **couldn't hardly** keep my eyes open.
Correct   I **couldn't** keep my eyes open.
Correct   I could **hardly** keep my eyes open.

Incorrect   I **haven't** done **nothing** all day.
Correct   I **haven't** done anything all day.
Correct   I have done **nothing** all day.

Prepositions, Conjunctions & Interjections

What Is a Preposition?

A **preposition** shows a relationship between words within a sentence. It relates a noun or a pronoun to another word in the sentence. The noun or pronoun that follows the preposition is called the **object of the preposition.**

>The cat is **on** the **chair.**

In the example sentence, the preposition *on* shows the relationship between the object of the preposition *chair* and the noun *cat*. To see this relationship more clearly, try changing the preposition in the sentence.

The cat is **behind** the chair.   The cat is **under** the chair.

Changing the preposition changes the relationship between *chair* and *cat*.

Common Prepositions

about	beneath	inside	since
above	beside	into	through
across	between	like	throughout
after	beyond	near	to
against	but	of	toward
along	by	off	under
among	down	on	underneath
around	during	onto	until
at	except	out	up
before	for	outside	upon
behind	from	over	with
below	in	past	without

Prepositional Phrases

In general, prepositions appear as part of prepositional phrases. A **prepositional phrase** is a group of words that begins with a preposition and ends with the object of the preposition. The object of the preposition may be a noun or a pronoun.

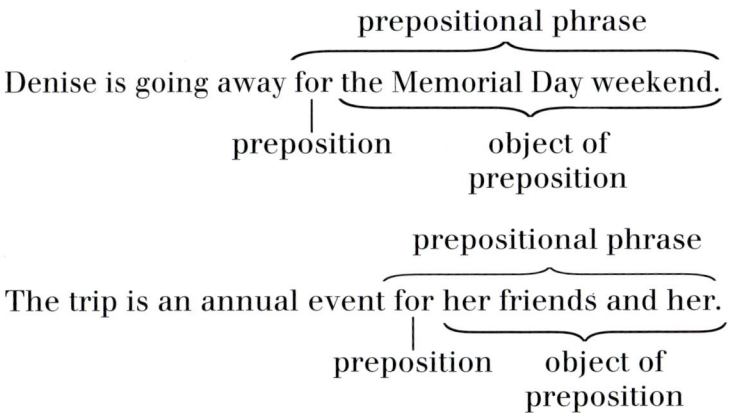

Note that in a prepositional phrase, one or more words may come between the preposition and the object. In the first example sentence, *the* and *Memorial Day* describe the object *weekend*. Words that describe the object are part of the prepositional phrase. Also, a preposition may have more than one object. In the second example sentence, the preposition has two objects: the noun *friends* and the pronoun *her*.

A sentence may have more than one prepositional phrase.

> **In the morning,** Denise will drive **to a state park** and camp **for three days.**

Prepositional phrases may follow one another in a sentence. This sentence has three prepositional phrases in a row.

> Her favorite camping place is **in the woods by the river near the cliffs.**

62 • Prepositions, Conjunctions & Interjections

Prepositional Phrases as Adjectives and Adverbs

Like adjectives and adverbs, prepositional phrases are used as modifiers.

A prepositional phrase that modifies a noun or a pronoun is called an **adjective phrase.** Like adjectives, an adjective phrase tells *what kind* or *which one* about the noun or pronoun it modifies.

> Novels **about faraway places** are Antonio's favorites.
> (*About faraway places* modifies the noun *novels*. The adjective phrase tells *what kind*.)

> He also reads books **from the travel section.**
> (*From the travel section* modifies the noun *books*. The adjective phrase tells *which ones*.)

A prepositional phrase that modifies a verb, an adjective, or an adverb is called an **adverb phrase.** Like adverbs, an adverb phrase tells *how, when, where,* or *how much* about the verb, adjective, or adverb it modifies.

> Antonio is happy **at the library.**
> (*At the library* modifies the adjective *happy*. The adverb phrase tells *where*.)

> Often he stays there and reads **for hours.**
> (*For hours* modifies the verb *reads*. The adverb phrase tells *how much*.)

> Antonio chooses his books **with great care.**
> (*With great care* modifies the verb *chooses*. The adverb phrase tells *how*.)

> He does most of his reading **on weekends.**
> (*On weekends* modifies the verb *does*. The adverb phrase tells *when*.)

See pages 47–48 for information on adjectives as modifiers and page 54 for information on adverbs as modifiers.

Prepositions, Conjunctions & Interjections • 63

Pronouns After Prepositions

Remember, only the object forms of personal pronouns can be used as the objects of verbs or the objects of prepositions. The object forms are *me, you, him, her, it, us,* and *them*.

Did Rachel give the letter **to him?**
Ed said the letter was **for her.**
I think the letter is **from them.**
Quinn wants to take the letter **with us.**

Sometimes a preposition has more than one object. If any of the objects are pronouns, the object forms of the pronouns must be used.

Trisha wrote a letter to Dad and **me.**
The letter from **you** and **him** arrived today.

To decide which pronoun form to use in sentences with more than one object, read the sentence with only the pronoun after the preposition.

Letters came from everyone but Jarod and _____.
<u>she, her</u>

Letters came from everyone but **her.**
Letters came from everyone but Jarod and **her.**

I wrote back to Trisha and _____.
<u>he, him</u>

I wrote back to **him.**
I wrote back to Trisha and **him.**

See pages 40–41 for information on using pronouns as objects.

Understanding Prepositions

Preposition or Adverb?

Some words, such as *by, up, down, in, out, around, above, over, inside,* and *outside,* can be used either as prepositions or as adverbs.

> Kenji glanced **up** as Alicia walked **by.** (adverbs)
> He glanced **up** the street as she walked **by** the door. (prepositions)
>
> When I went **out,** the dog ran **inside.** (adverbs)
> When I went **out** the door, it ran **inside** the house. (prepositions)
>
> Hal looked **around** and then climbed **down.** (adverbs)
> He looked **around** the attic and then climbed **down** the ladder. (prepositions)

How can you tell whether the word is a preposition or an adverb? If the word begins a phrase and is followed by a noun or a pronoun, it is probably a preposition. A preposition is always followed by its object. If the word is used alone, it is probably an adverb.

See page 54 for information about adverbs.

Confusing Prepositions

Writers sometimes confuse the following pairs of prepositions, using one when they should use the other. The information and examples found on the next page can help you use the prepositions correctly.

Prepositions, Conjunctions & Interjections • 65

Between–Among

Between is used to refer to two people, things, or groups.

> On the bus, Gerald sat **between** Kathy and Mark.
> The bus stalled **between** Adams St. and Monroe Blvd.

Among is used to refer to three or more people, things, or groups.

> Hannah wandered **among** the museum displays.
> **Among** the four of us, we saw all the major exhibits.

Beside–Besides

Beside means "by the side of."

> At lunch, Hannah sat **beside** Gerald.
> Kathy put her lunchbox on the seat **beside** her.

Besides means "in addition to."

> What are you having for lunch **besides** juice?
> No one **besides** Mark will eat tofu.

From–Off

From can mean "out of the possession of." *Off* does not have that meaning. Do not use *off* when you mean *from*.

Incorrect   Hannah got a dollar **off** Mark.
Correct   Hannah got a dollar **from** Mark.

In–Into

In means "within or inside something."

> Kathy saw dinosaur skeletons **in** the museum.
> Gerald has a dinosaur book **in** his backpack.

Into indicates movement from the outside to the inside.

> How did they get those skeletons **into** the museum?
> Gerald put the book **into** his backpack.

Conjunctions

What Is a Conjunction?

A **conjunction** is a word that is used to join words or groups of words.

Common Conjunctions

The most common conjunctions are *and, but, or, nor, so,* and *yet.* These conjunctions are used to join subjects, verbs, objects, and sentences and make them into compounds.

To make a compound subject:

>Barbara likes movies. Tim likes movies.
>Barbara **and** Tim like movies.

To make a compound verb:

>Barbara rents movies. Barbara buys movies.
>Barbara rents **and** buys movies.

To make a compound object:

>Barbara collects movies. Barbara collects CDs.
>Barbara collects movies **and** CDs.

When two sentences are joined by a conjunction to make a compound sentence, a comma is placed at the end of the first sentence before the conjunction.

To make a compound sentence:

>Barbara likes dramas. Tim prefers science fiction.
>Barbara likes dramas, **but** Tim prefers science fiction.

When three or more subjects, verbs, or objects are joined by a conjunction, commas are placed after all the items but the last one.

>Barbara, Tim, **and** Jeremy go to the movies together.
>Movies make them smile, laugh, **or** cry.

Conjunction Pairs

Some conjunctions are used in pairs to join words or groups of words. Here are these conjunction pairs:

either... or   not only... but also
neither... nor whether... or
both... and

Either Barbara **or** Tim will choose a movie.
They debate **whether** to go now **or** to wait until later.
Barbara and Tim like **both** westerns **and** comedies.
Neither she **nor** he likes horror movies.
They watch movies **not only** at theaters **but also** on TV.

Conjunctions and Clauses

Some conjunctions join main and dependent clauses in sentences. A **main clause** has a subject and a verb and can stand alone as a sentence. A **dependent clause** has a subject and a verb but cannot stand alone as a sentence.

Dependent clause   **After** the movie was over
Main clause   they went home
Complete sentence   **After** the movie was over, they went home.

Some conjunctions that begin dependent clauses and join them to main clauses are

after   as though   if   until
although   because   since   when
as   before   than   where
as if   even though unless   while

When Jeremy comes over, we will watch a movie.
I chose the movie **while** I was at the video store.
Since I have a VCR, we met at my house.
Let me get the popcorn **before** we start the movie.

Interjections

What Is an Interjection?

An **interjection** is a word or phrase used to express strong feeling.

An interjection might be used to express surprise, horror, excitement, anger, joy, fear, amazement, pain, or disgust. Here are some interjections:

    Oh!   **Ah!**   **Well!**   **Wow!**
    Oops!   **Ouch!**   **Help!**   **Hey!**

An interjection used alone with an exclamation point is functioning as an exclamatory sentence. The interjections above are exclamatory sentences. Remember, an exclamatory sentence expresses strong feeling and indicates this by ending with an exclamation point.

Usually interjections are used as part of a sentence. Sometimes they are separated from the sentence by an exclamation point, a question mark, or a period. The first word of the rest of the sentence is capitalized.

    Not again! How could I be so clumsy?
    Really? You're sure it doesn't hurt?
    Great! I'm so relieved you're all right.

Sometimes interjections are separated from the rest of the sentence by a comma. The first word after the comma is not capitalized.

    My, that bread smells good!
    Hey, who took the last slice?
    Gee, you can't trust anyone around fresh bread.

Words that are commonly used as other parts of speech can be used as interjections. Adjectives, verbs, and adverbs, can all be used as interjections.

    Unbelievable! Did you see her last dive?
    Wait! The judges are giving their scores.
    Never! I can't believe there are no 6's!

See page 14 for information on exclamatory sentences.

Subject-Verb Agreement

Prepositional Phrases in Subjects

Sometimes the subject of a sentence may be followed by a prepositional phrase. Because the prepositional phrase is between the subject and the verb, and the object of the preposition is closer to the verb than the subject, writers often become confused. They mistakenly make the verb agree with the object rather than the subject.

> The **price** of most daily newspapers **is** 50 cents.
> The **necklace** with diamonds and pearls **costs** too much.

What is the subject of the first sentence? *Price* is. *Price* is singular, so the verb *is* is singular. *Of most daily newspapers* is a prepositional phrase. *Newspapers* is the object of the preposition *of*. It is not the subject of the sentence. The object of a preposition can never be the subject of a sentence. Similarly, *necklace* is the subject of the second sentence. The verb agrees with *necklace*, not with *diamonds and pearls*.

Compound Subjects with Conjunctions

When two or more subjects are joined by the conjunction *and*, use the plural form of the verb.

> Ben and Ellen **are** newspaper reporters.
> Ben, Ellen, and Theo **write** local news stories.

To make sure you are using the correct verb form, say the sentence using a pronoun for the subject.

> **They are** newspaper reporters.
> **They write** local news stories.

When two or more subjects are joined by the conjunctions *or, either/or,* or *neither/nor,* use the form of the verb that agrees with the subject that is closest to the verb. In other words, if the subject closest to the verb is singular, the verb is singular. If that subject is plural, the verb is plural.

> The mayor or council members **are** speaking today.
> Either a reporter or a photographer **is** at the meeting.
> Neither her writing nor his photos **tell** the whole story.

70 • Prepositions, Conjunctions & Interjections

Parts of Speech

Using Words as Different Parts of Speech

What part of speech a word is depends on how the word is used in a sentence.

> The skyscraper towered **above** our heads.
> The skyscraper towered **above**.

The word *above* is used as a preposition in the first sentence. But how is it used in the second sentence? It is used as an adverb.

> **That** building is the tallest in the world.
> **That** is a very tall building.

The word *that* is used as an adjective in the first sentence. But how is it used in the second sentence? It is used as a pronoun.

You already know that words such as *above* and *that* can be two different parts of speech. Many other words can function as more than one part of speech. How a word is used in a sentence determines what part of speech the word is.

Each year the city hosts a 10-kilometer **race.**

Runners **race** through the city streets.

How is *race* used in the first sentence? It is used as a noun. It names a thing and it receives the action of the verb *hosts*. How is *race* used in the second sentence? It is used as a verb. It expresses an action. Same word, two different parts of speech.

Mechanics

The word "mechanics" refers to capitalization and punctuation. Using capital letters and punctuation correctly in your writing will help you get your ideas across clearly.

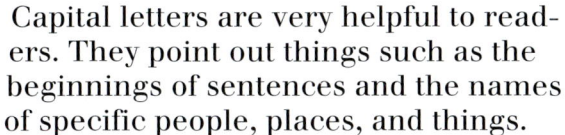

Capital letters are very helpful to readers. They point out things such as the beginnings of sentences and the names of specific people, places, and things.

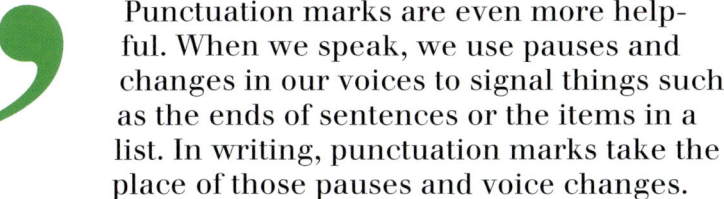

Punctuation marks are even more helpful. When we speak, we use pauses and changes in our voices to signal things such as the ends of sentences or the items in a list. In writing, punctuation marks take the place of those pauses and voice changes.

It makes sense to learn how to use punctuation marks and capital letters correctly. Incorrect punctuation and capitalization will confuse or mislead your readers. When you use mechanics well, your readers get your meaning quickly and accurately, which, after all, is what you want.

This section explains the rules governing capitalization and punctuation in English. You will learn about the rules that must be followed and the situations in which the writer has a choice. The explanations are accompanied by examples to show you clearly when and how to use capitals and punctuation marks in your own writing.

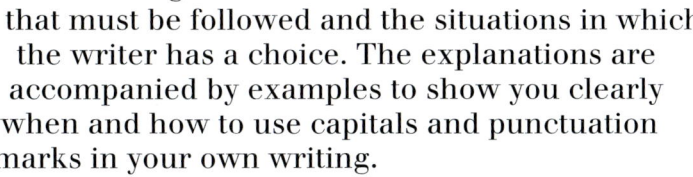

Capitalization

Proper Nouns and Adjectives

Remember, a proper noun names a particular person, place, thing, or idea. A proper adjective is an adjective that is made by adding an ending to a proper noun. Proper nouns and proper adjectives are always capitalized. That is, they always begin with capital letters. Common nouns and common adjectives are not capitalized.

Common Noun	**Common Adjective**
city	urban
country	rural

Proper Noun	**Proper Adjective**
Paris	**P**arisian
China	**C**hinese

Proper nouns can be more than one word. Capitalize all the important words.

    Gulf of **M**exico   **D**eclaration of **I**ndependence

Here are some rules for capitalizing words:

People's Names and Titles

• Capitalize the first, last, and middle names of people. Capitalize their initials, too. Remember to put a period after an initial.

    Barbara **J**ordan
    Ruth **B**ader **G**insberg
    John **F**. **K**ennedy
    J. **P**aul **G**etty
    J.**R**.**R**. **T**olkien
    Susan **B**. **A**nthony

- Capitalize personal titles used with people's names. Capitalize a title whether it is written as a whole word or as an abbreviation. Remember to put a period after an abbreviation.

    Mister Jorsky   Doctor Weiner   Professor Wong
    Mr. Jorsky   Dr. Weiner   Prof. Wong

    Captain Ellison   Senator Sanchez   Reverend Canby
    Capt. Ellison   Sen. Sanchez
    Rev. Canby

- Do not capitalize a title when it is used alone or after a person's name.

> The doctor is with Jay Wong, professor of economics.
> Ann Sanchez, senator from Arizona, is standing next to the captain.

- Capitalize these titles when they are used with names or when they are used alone to refer to the people who currently hold the positions.

    the President   President Washington
    (of the United States)
    the Vice-President   Vice-President Johnson
    (of the United States)
    the Pope   Pope John Paul II

Pronoun I

- Capitalize the pronoun *I*.

> Aunt Sue told me that I had grown.
> She says that every time, and I just smile.

Days, Months, Holidays, and Seasons

- Capitalize the names of days, months, and holidays. Do not capitalize the names of the seasons.

> The fourth Thursday in November is Thanksgiving.
> Valentine's Day is Monday, February 14.
> The Fourth of July is a major summer holiday.

74 • Capitalization

Geographical Names

- Capitalize the names of places and things, including

  Continents—North America, Asia, Europe, Africa
  Countries—India, Canada, Spain, South Korea
  States/Provinces—Oregon, Manitoba, Rhode Island
  Cities/Towns—Tokyo, San Antonio, Moose Jaw
  Mountains—Rocky Mountains, the Himalayas, Appalachian Mountains
  Oceans—Arctic Ocean, Indian Ocean
  Lakes—Lake Michigan, Lake Victoria, Crater Lake
  Rivers—Nile River, Amazon River
  Parks—Zion National Park, Starved Rock State Park
  Buildings—Empire State Building, Eiffel Tower
  Streets—Madison Avenue, Sunset Boulevard
  Highways—Interstate 57, Natchez Trace Parkway
  Monuments—Lincoln Memorial, Washington Monument
  Bridges—Golden Gate Bridge, Sydney Harbour Bridge

Nationalities, Languages, and Religions

- Capitalize the names of nationalities, languages, and religions.

Mexican	Swahili	Islam
Irish	Gaelic	Catholicism
American	Yiddish	Hinduism

Religious Names and Terms

- Capitalize religious names and terms, such as names for God and religious writings.

God	Lord	Koran	Veda
Allah	Vishnu	Bible	Torah

Historical Events and Documents

- Capitalize the names of historical events and documents.

> Battle of Gettysburg
> French Revolution
> Constitutional Convention
> Crimean War
> Magna Carta
> Voting Rights Act
> Treaty of Versailles
> Bill of Rights

Businesses, Organizations, and Institutions

- Capitalize the names of businesses, organizations, and institutions, including schools, colleges, clubs, political parties, government agencies, and museums.

> United Airlines
> Shell Oil Company
> University of Wisconsin
> Cambridge University
> National Park Service
> Smithsonian Institution
> Uffizi Palace
> American Heart Association
> National Geographic Society
> Rotary International
> Sierra Club
> General Accounting Office
> Democratic Party
> African National Congress

Planes, Trains, Ships, and Spacecraft

- Capitalize the names of planes, trains, ships, and spacecraft.

> the *Spirit of St. Louis*
> HMS *Victory*
> the *Twentieth Century Limited*
> *Galileo*
> the *Santa María*
> *Viking II*

See page 17 for information on proper nouns, page 48 for information on proper adjectives, and pages 79–80 for information on punctuating abbreviations and initials.

76 • Capitalization

First Words

Sentences

• Capitalize the first word of every sentence, whether the sentence is declarative, interrogative, imperative, or exclamatory.

> **M**any people think a robin is a sign of spring.
> **H**ow fast can a hummingbird fly?
> **P**lease do not feed the toucans.
> **W**hat a beautiful color flamingos are!

Quotations

• Capitalize the first word of a direct quotation. A **direct quotation** is the repeating of a person's exact words. The first word of the quotation is capitalized.

> "**D**id you see that bird?" asked Emma.
> She exclaimed, "**I**t was a scarlet tanager!"

• In a **divided quotation,** words such as *she said* or *he asked* divide the quotation into two parts. These words are called speaker's tags. The first word in the second part is capitalized *only* if it begins a new sentence.

> "**I** saw it," said Kate. "**T**hat bird was a cardinal."
> "**A** cardinal has red wings," argued Emma, "and that bird had black wings."

See page 14 for information on kinds of sentences. See page 87 and pages 92–93 for information on punctuating quotations.

Poems

• Capitalize the first word in each line of poetry.

> **T**he **E**agle
>
> **H**e clasps the crag with crooked hands:
> **C**lose to the sun in lonely lands,
> **R**inged with the azure world, he stands.
> **T**he wrinkled sea beneath him crawls:
> **H**e watches from his mountain walls,
> **A**nd like a thunderbolt he falls.
> —*Alfred, Lord Tennyson*

Sometimes, particularly in modern poems, the lines of a poem do not begin with capital letters. To capitalize or not is the poet's choice. When you quote part of a poem, you should use the same capitalization that the poet does.

Outlines

• Capitalize the first word in every line of an outline. Capitalize the letters that indicate sections.

> **B**irds
> I. **K**ind of animal
>   **A.** **V**ariety and range
>   **B.** **F**ossil history
> II. **S**tructure and function
>   **A.** **F**eathers
>   **B.** **W**ings
>   **C.** **L**egs
> III. **B**ehaviors
>   **A.** **M**ating and breeding
>   1. **T**erritory
>   2. **N**ests
>   **B.** **F**eeding

Note that Roman numerals (I, II, III) indicate the major divisions, capital letters (A, B, C) indicate the next level of divisions, and Arabic numerals (1, 2) indicate the level of divisions after that.

To Capitalize or Not?

Titles

• Capitalize the first and last words of a title and all other words except articles, short conjunctions, and short prepositions such as *of, for,* and *with.*

>*U.S. News and World Report* (magazine)
>*All Quiet on the Western Front* (book)
>*A Raisin in the Sun* (play)
>*Dances with Wolves* (movie)
>"A Rose for Emily" (short story)
>"Nothing Can Stay Gold" (poem)
>"The Battle Hymn of the Republic" (song)

Family Relationships

• Capitalize words used to name family relationships *only* when they are used as names. Do not capitalize them if they follow an article (*a, an, the*) or a possessive adjective, such as *her* or *his.*

>Alex met Dad and Aunt Sue at the train.
>Alex met her father and her aunt at the train.

Sections vs. Directions

• Capitalize *north, south, east,* and *west* and their adjective forms when they refer to areas of the country or world. Do not capitalize the words when they refer to directions.

>Doug was born in the East but moved to the West. He liked Eastern cities but preferred the Western climate.
>To get to Phoenix, he traveled west on Interstate 10. It follows a southern route across the country.

See page 94 for information on punctuating titles.

Punctuation

Period

Here are some rules about when to use a period (.):

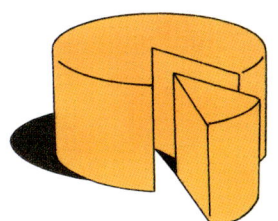

- Use a period at the end of a declarative sentence. Remember, a declarative sentence makes a statement.

   We are making a casserole for dinner.
   It has noodles, cheese, and broccoli in it.

- Use a period at the end of *most* imperative sentences. Remember, an imperative sentence gives a command or makes a request.

   Hand me that cup of milk, please.
   Set the temperature of the oven at 375°.

When an imperative sentence expresses strong feeling, use an exclamation point at the end of the sentence.

   Be careful with the boiling water!

- Use a period after an abbreviation. Remember, an abbreviation is a shortened form of a word.

tbsp.	tablespoon	Jr.	Junior
oz.	ounce	St.	Street
Tues.	Tuesday	Ave.	Avenue
Sept.	September	hr.	hour
Dr.	Doctor	min.	minute

Some abbreviations do not have periods.

m	meter
g	gram
mph	miles per hour
AL	Alabama
KS	Kansas
DVD	digital video disc
FBI	Federal Bureau of Investigation

Some abbreviations may be written with or without periods. It is always a good idea to check a dictionary to see whether to use periods in an abbreviation. Also, except for a few abbreviations, do not use abbreviations in formal writing. However, you should use abbreviations for titles in formal writing.

- Use a period after an initial. Remember, an initial is the first letter of a name.

    Fannie M. Farmer   Fannie Merritt Farmer
    G. A. Escoffier   Georges Auguste Escoffier

- Use a period after each number separating items in a list.

    Shopping List
    1. egg noodles, 10 oz.
    2. shredded cheddar cheese, 6 oz.
    3. fresh broccoli, ½ lb.
    4. 2% milk

- Use a period after each number or letter separating items in an outline.

    Cooking
    I. Earliest types of cooking
        A. Advances in cooking techniques
        B. Cooking in ancient societies
            1. Egypt
            2. Greece
    II. Development of modern cuisines
        A. Medieval cookery
            1. Northern Europe
            2. Italy
        B. Emergence of French cuisine
        C. Chinese influence
        D. American cuisines
            1. New foods
            2. Technology

See page 14 for information on declarative and imperative sentences, pages 72–73 for information on capitalizing initials and abbreviations, and page 77 for information on capitalizing outlines.

Question Mark and Exclamation Point

Here are some rules about when to use a question mark (?) or an exclamation point (!):

Question Mark

• Use a question mark at the end of an interrogative sentence. Remember, an interrogative sentence asks a question.

> How many games has this basketball team won?
> Did you see that last basket by Taylor?

Exclamation Point

• Use an exclamation point at the end of an exclamatory sentence. Remember, an exclamatory sentence expresses strong feeling.

> That was an incredible field goal!
> I can't believe the referee called a foul!

• Use an exclamation point at the end of an imperative sentence if the sentence gives a strong command.

Block that shot!   Stop that guy!
Get the ball back!   Don't miss!

• Use an exclamation point after an interjection. Remember, an interjection is a word or phrase used to express strong feeling.

Wow!   Great game!   Amazing!

See page 14 for information on kinds of sentences. See page 68 for information on interjections.

Comma

Using Commas to Set Off

Commas (,) are used to set off a particular part of a sentence from the rest of the sentence. Setting off the part makes the sentence easier to read and understand.

Introductory Words

Use commas after words such as *yes, no,* and *well* when they are used at the beginning of a sentence.

> Yes, I did lose my favorite black pen.
> No, that black pen is not the one.
> Well, I have looked for it everywhere.
> My, there are certainly a lot of pens in this office!
> Oh, I think I see my pen under that desk.

Direct Address

Use commas in **direct address,** that is, when someone is speaking in direct address. Place a comma after the name of a person spoken to when the name appears at the beginning of a sentence. Place a comma before the name when it appears at the end of a sentence. Place commas before and after the name when it appears in the middle of a sentence.

> Andy, did you take the last box of paper clips?
> There are plenty of paper clips in that drawer, Herb.
> But, Andy, do those clips have a plastic coating?
> You'll have to look at them, Herb, to see if they do.

Omitting the commas in direct address can affect the meaning of a sentence.

> Andy put the report in my office.
> Andy, put the report in my office.

The first sentence states an action that Andy has done. The second sentence is a request addressed to Andy. The comma makes the difference.

Appositives

Appositives add information about something in the sentence. An appositive follows a noun and gives more information about the noun. Because they only add information, most appositives can be taken out of their sentences without changing the meaning of the sentences.

Use commas to set off most appositives. Place a comma before an appositive at the end of a sentence. Place commas before and after an appositive in the middle of a sentence.

> Helen**,** our office manager**,** orders the supplies.
> She gets them from Elwood's**,** a local company.
> On Friday**,** the busiest day of the week**,** we always seem to run out of paper.

Some appositives, however, are needed to make the meaning clear. These appositives are not set off with commas.

> The writer Nathaniel Hawthorne worked in an office.
> "How could he work and write?" asks my friend Amy.

Words and Phrases that Interrupt

Words and phrases such as *I think, however,* and *of course* are called **interrupters** because they interrupt the flow of a sentence. They may be used at the beginning or in the middle of a sentence. Use commas before and after interrupters.

> It would be hard**,** I think**,** to work full time and write.
> However**,** people have done both successfully.
> It would be easier**,** of course**,** to do one or the other.

Here is a list of some common interrupters:

after all	of course	indeed
by the way	for example	however
in fact	incidentally	therefore
I suppose	I believe	I think

Using Commas to Separate

Commas are used to separate words or ideas in sentences. These commas help readers more easily read and understand the sentences.

In a Series

Use commas to separate three or more items in a series. Place a comma after each item except the last one.

> Glenn, Alicia, and Dave are planning a party.
> They design, write, and send their own invitations.

They plan to have recorded music, videos, and games.

Omitting a comma in a series can affect the meaning of a sentence.

> Carlos, Mary, Anne, and Dennis are coming.
> Carlos, Mary Anne, and Dennis are coming.

In the first sentence, four people are coming to the party. In the second sentence, three people are coming to the party. A comma makes the difference.

With Adjectives

Use commas to separate two or more adjectives that modify the same noun.

> Alicia wants to decorate with big, silver balloons.
> Dave prefers to use long, colorful, plastic streamers.

Do not use a comma before the last adjective if that adjective is considered to be part of the noun.

> But Alicia is a determined young woman.
> (No comma before *young* because *young* is considered to be part of *woman.*)

> Balloons will decorate the cold, dark basement walls.
> (No comma before *basement* because *basement* is considered to be part of *walls.*)

In Compound Sentences

Use commas before conjunctions such as *and, but,* and *or* when these words are used to combine sentences.

> They can order pizzas, **or** they can order sandwiches.
> They talk about it, **and** they decide to order both.

To Include or Exclude

Use commas to separate information that is not needed to understand the sentence.

> Glenn**,** who has planned many parties**,** thinks this party will be a big success.
> Glenn is the only one of the three who has planned many parties.

In the first sentence, the clause *who has planned many parties* adds information to the sentence, but it is not necessary to the basic meaning of the sentence *Glenn thinks this party will be a big success.* So the clause is separated from the rest of the sentence by commas.

In the second sentence, the clause *who has planned many parties* is necessary. Without the clause, the meaning of the sentence changes. So the clause is not separated from the rest of the sentence by a comma.

To decide whether a clause should be separated by commas, try saying the sentence without the clause. If the sentence still makes sense, the clause probably needs commas.

To Make Meaning Clear

Use commas to make the meaning of a sentence clear and to avoid confusing the reader.

> When he called Glenn wanted to talk about the music.
> When he called**,** Glenn wanted to talk about the music.
> He had his CDs and his player was in the car.
> He had his CDs**,** and his player was in the car.

In each example, a comma keeps the reader from misreading the sentence and helps make the meaning clear.

Conventional Uses of Commas

Sometimes, using commas does not have much to do with meaning. In these cases, it is customary in English to use a comma in a certain place. These are **conventional** uses of commas. It is important for you to understand the conventional use of commas. Your readers expect to see commas in certain places and will be distracted if commas are not used correctly in these situations.

Dates

Use commas between the parts of a date. Place a comma before the year.

Pablo was born in Los Angeles on April 10, 1988.
On August 16, 1994, his family moved to Canada.
Pablo remembers November 2, 1994, very well because that was the day he saw snow for the first time.

Note that when a date appears in the middle of a sentence, a comma is also placed after the year.

No comma is used if the date has only a month and a year.

They moved back to the United States in May 2000.

Addresses

Use commas between parts of addresses. Place a comma between the name of a city or town and the name of a state or country.

Los Angeles, California   Toronto, Canada

When an address appears in a sentence, place a comma after each part except between the name of the state and the zip code.

Pablo went to college in Chicago, Illinois, and medical school in Miami, Florida. Now his mail is addressed to Dr. Pablo J. Herrera, 560 14th Street, Brooklyn, NY 11218.

Letters

Use a comma after the greeting in a friendly letter. Use a comma after the closing in a friendly or business letter.

>Dear Pablo,   Dear Mama,
>Love,   Your son,
>Sincerely yours,   Respectfully,

Quotations

Use commas to set off speaker's tags from direct quotations.

Remember, a **direct quotation** is the repeating of a person's exact words. Quotation marks are placed before and after the quotation. Phrases such as *he said* and *she asked* are called **speaker's tags**.

>Mama asked, "When are you coming for a visit?"
>"I'll come for your birthday," Pablo replied.

In the first sentence, the speaker's tag *Mama asked* is at the beginning of the sentence. So a comma is placed after the last word of the speaker's tag. In the second sentence, the speaker's tag *Pablo replied* is at the end of the sentence. So a comma is placed between the last word of the quotation *and* the closing quotation mark.

In a divided quotation, the speaker's tag divides the quotation into two parts.

>"My birthday," said Mama, "is three months away."

A comma is placed after the last word in the first part of the quotation *and* inside the quotation marks. A comma is also placed after the last word of the speaker's tag.

You can learn more about punctuating quotations on pages 92–93. See page 76 for information on capitalizing quotations.

Semicolon and Colon

Semicolons (;), like commas, separate parts of sentences. But a semicolon indicates a more definite break than a comma does. Colons (:) signal an even stronger break. A colon usually points to what comes next.

Semicolon

- Use a semicolon between two related sentences.

Two related sentences can be combined using a comma and a conjunction such as *and, but,* or *or.* The sentences can also be combined using a semicolon. The semicolon takes the place of the comma and the conjunction.

> Chris tosses the ball up, **and** her racquet smacks it hard.
> Chris tosses the ball up**;** her racquet smacks it hard.
>
> The ball goes right to Ivan, **but** he swings and misses it.
> The ball goes right to Ivan**;** he swings and misses it.

- Use semicolons and certain conjunctions between two related sentences.

Two related sentences can be combined using one of the following conjunctions: *accordingly, also, besides, furthermore, however, instead, moreover, nevertheless, otherwise, therefore.* A semicolon is placed before the conjunction, and a comma is placed after the conjunction.

> Ivan has a good backhand**; however,** he needs to work on his serve.
> Chris has a powerful serve**; furthermore,** she rarely hits the ball into the net.

- Use semicolons between items in a series when there are commas in the items.

> Spectators at the game include Chris's mother, who is also a tennis player**;** Ivan's father, who once played at Wimbledon**;** and Ivan's younger brother.

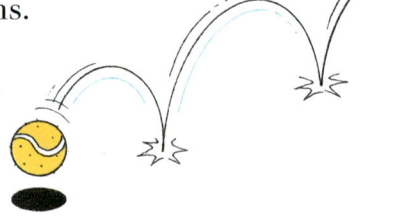

Colon

- Use a colon after the greeting in a business letter.

    Dear Sir: Dear Mrs. Tanaka:
    Dear Customer Service Representative:

- Use a colon between the numbers for hours and minutes in a time expression.

    8:15 A.M.   12:05 P.M.   10:28 P.M.

The abbreviations A.M. and P.M., which are used in time expressions, stand for *ante meridiem,* meaning "before noon," and *post meridiem,* meaning "after noon." Capitalize both letters and put a period after each letter.

- Use a colon before a list of items. The colon indicates "note what follows."

Usually, the colon follows a noun or a pronoun. Do not use a colon after a verb or a preposition that introduces a list.

> Chris packed a can of tennis balls, an extra pair of socks, a towel, and a water bottle in her gym bag.

> Chris packed the following items in her gym bag: a can of tennis balls, an extra pair of socks, a towel, and a water bottle.

> Before a match, Ivan does these activities: leg stretches, curl-ups, bicep curls, and deep breathing exercises.

> Before a match, Ivan likes to stretch his legs, do curl-ups and bicep curls, and practice deep breathing.

See page 85 for information on using commas in compound sentences. See page 87 for information on punctuating the closing in a friendly or business letter.

Apostrophe and Hyphen

Apostrophe

- Use apostrophes to form the possessive forms of nouns.

For a singular noun, add an apostrophe and an *s* at the end of the noun.

    Heather's apartment   Boss's doghouse
    the van's carport   the bus's garage

For a plural noun that ends in *s*, add an apostrophe.

    the Garcias' ranch   the Larsons' farm
    the frogs' pond   the lions' den

For a plural noun that does not end in *s*, add an apostrophe and an *s*.

    the people's houses   the children's cabins
    the geese's nest   the oxen's barn

- For more than one noun, add an apostrophe and an *s* to the second noun if both nouns have ownership of the thing that is possessed. In the examples below, both Andy and Beth have the same dog. Grandma and Grandpa have the same house.

    Andy and Beth's dog   Grandma and Grandpa's house

If the nouns have ownership of different things, add an apostrophe and an *s* to both nouns.

In the examples below, Stephen and Cathy have different dogs. Aunt Mia and Aunt Janet do not have the same house.

    Stephen's and   Aunt Mia's and Aunt
    Cathy's dogs   Janet's houses

- Use apostrophes to form the plurals of numbers, letters, signs, and words used as words.

    To form these plurals, add an apostrophe and an *s*.

    8's, not *3*'s   dot the *i*'s and *j*'s
    +'s and -'s   no *if*'s, *and*'s, or *but*'s

- Use apostrophes in contractions.

A contraction is made of two words joined together with one or more letters left out. An apostrophe shows where the letter or letters have been omitted. Here is a list of common contractions:

I am—I'm	you have—you've	can not—can't
you are—you're	she had—she'd	do not—don't
it is—it's	we will—we'll	did not—didn't
we are—we're	is not—isn't	has not—hasn't
they are—they're	are not—aren't	have not—haven't
I have—I've	was not—wasn't	will not—won't

Hyphen

- Use hyphens in compound numbers from twenty-one to ninety-nine and in fractions.

> thirty-one cousins eighty-six votes
> two-thirds of the relatives one-eighth of the voters

- Use hyphens in some compound words.

A **compound word** is made up of two or more smaller words. Some compound words are written as one word, some are written as separate words, and some are written with hyphens between the words. Look up a compound word in a dictionary to see whether it needs a hyphen.

> Our great-aunt lives with my brother and sister-in-law. Even though she is now the ex-mayor, she has not lost her self-confidence.

- Use hyphens to divide words at the end of lines.

When dividing a word at the end of a line, place a hyphen after the first part of the word and then write the second part of the word on the next line. Always divide the word between syllables. Do not divide a one-syllable word. Use a dictionary to find out how a word is divided into syllables.

> At 82, she worked harder than many younger candi-dates did on the campaign trail.

92 • Punctuation

Quotation Marks

When you write what someone has said, you are quoting the person or writing a **quotation.** If you write exactly what the person says, you are writing a **direct quotation.** If you do not write exactly what the person says, you are writing an **indirect quotation.**

Direct Quotations   She said, "I want to go."
He asked, "Why do you want to go?"

Indirect Quotations   She said that she wanted to go.
He asked why she wanted to go.

In a direct quotation, quotation marks are used to show which words the person said. A phrase such as *she said* or *he asked* used in a direct quotation is called a **speaker's tag.** No quotation marks are used in an indirect quotation.

• Use quotation marks before and after the words of a direct quotation.

Sheila declared, "The amusement park would be fun."

"I'm not so sure about that," Bert groaned.

• When the speaker's tag is at the beginning of a sentence, a comma is placed after the speaker's tag.

Sheila said, "I like the really fast, high rides."
Bert muttered, "I like the slow, low ones."

• When the speaker's tag is at the end of the sentence, a comma is placed after the quotation inside the quotation marks.

"I've seen you ride the roller coaster," insisted Sheila.

"You've seen me ride it only once," replied Bert.

- When a quotation is at the end of a sentence, and the quotation ends with a period, question mark, or exclamation point, place the end punctuation mark inside the quotation marks.

> Sheila said, "I could ride it again and again."
> She asked, "Why don't you like the fast rides?"
> Bert answered, "Because they make me sick!"

- When a quotation is at the beginning of a sentence, and the quotation ends with a question mark or an exclamation point, place the end punctuation mark inside the quotation marks.

> "Did they make you dizzy and queasy?" asked Sheila.
> "But that's why the rides are fun!" she exclaimed.

- When a question mark or an exclamation point belongs to the sentence and *not* to the quotation, place the end punctuation mark outside the quotation marks.

> Did Bert actually say, "You're crazy, Sheila"?
> How astounding to hear Bert say, "OK, I'll go"!

A direct quotation that is divided into two parts is called a **divided quotation.** In a divided quotation, the speaker's tag is in the middle of the quotation.

> "Sitting in the front seat of the first car," said Sheila, "is the only way to ride a roller coaster!"
> "My head hurts," moaned Bert. "I think I left my stomach back on the first loop."

Quotation marks are used to mark both parts of the quotation. A comma is placed after the words in the first part of the quotation. In the first example sentence, a comma is placed after the speaker's tag because the second part of the quotation is *not* a new sentence. In the second example sentence, a period is placed after the speaker's tag because the second part of the quotation is a new sentence.

See page 76 for information on capitalizing direct quotations and page 87 for information on using commas in direct quotations.

Punctuating Titles

- Use quotation marks around the titles of short stories, poems, songs, essays, chapters of books, and articles in magazines or newspapers.

>"The Tell-Tale Heart" (short story)
>"Ode to the West Wind" (poem)
>"Auld Lang Syne" (song)
>"Civil Disobedience" (essay)
>Chapter 3, "The Solar System" (chapter)
>"Vietnam: The Ascending Dragon" (article)

When a title is written in a sentence, a period or comma after the title is placed inside the quotation marks. A semicolon or colon is placed outside the quotation marks.

>Our assignment is to read Chapter 4, "The Earth."
>Read "The Cask of Amontillado"; it is a scary story.

If a question mark or an exclamation point is part of a title, it is placed inside the quotation marks. If the question mark or exclamation point is not part of the title, it is placed outside the quotation marks.

>The funniest article in the magazine was "Help! I'm Caught in the Internet!"
>Did you read the humorous essay "You Can't Catch a Computer Virus"?

- Underline the titles of books, magazines, newspapers, plays, movies, and TV series.

>Sarah, Plain and Tall (book)
>Newsweek (magazine)
>The Wall Street Journal (newspaper)
>Romeo and Juliet (play)
>Raiders of the Lost Ark (movie)
>The Brady Bunch (TV series)

In printed materials, these titles appear in **italics.** Italics are slanted letters: *Beauty and the Beast.*

See page 78 for information on capitalizing titles.

Writing

Every writer has his or her own ways of writing. But to be able to talk about writing, it is necessary to choose one possible way to write, even as we recognize that writing is different for every writer and indeed for every kind of writing.

In this section, we will first discuss the writing process. By breaking the process into five possible stages, we can talk about what is involved in writing, from the idea to the finished product. The section explains these stages of the writing process, stressing how the stages are related to each other. Actually, the stages of writing function more like a circle (each stage leading back as well as forward) than a line (each stage as one definite step). We will offer help and suggestions in everything from finding ideas to writing a good beginning to sharing your writing with others. Use these suggestions if you need to. In time and with practice, you will discover your own ways of writing.

You will also learn some skills that can be useful when writing or working on any assignment. Finding the right word when you are writing can be very important. A dictionary or a thesaurus can be helpful in this quest. This section discusses how to use both of these reference sources. Spelling words correctly is also an important writing skill. We suggest ways you can improve your spelling ability, from keeping a list of troublesome words to remembering a few key rules. You will also find a list of some commonly confused words with meanings and sentences to help you use the words correctly.

The Writing Process

Five Stages of the Writing Process

Words like "process" and "stages" may make writing sound like something very mechanical. Actually, writing is anything but mechanical. But the idea of a process and stages helps when discussing what is involved in writing. Usually, the stages come up in the following order.

Prewriting. *The writer looks for a topic to write about and information on the topic.* Prewriting, as the name says, takes place *before* any writing. The task at this stage is to decide what you want to write about. Do anything that helps you make that choice. Perhaps you get ideas from reading, playing music, doodling on paper, or talking to someone.

Drafting. *The writer puts his or her ideas down on paper.* When writing a draft, you let your ideas flow and see what happens. Concentrate on getting down what you want to say. When you have finished a draft, put it aside and look at it again later. Also, having others read or listen to your draft can be helpful.

Revising. *The writer tries to improve what he or she has written.* Based on your own evaluation or the responses of others, you may decide to add or take out information, change the order of sentences or paragraphs, or replace words.

Proofreading. *The writer checks his or her writing for errors in spelling, punctuation, capitalization, and grammar.* Now that you have finished your revisions, it is time to look for and correct spelling errors and other mistakes before making your final copy.

Publishing. *The writer shares his or her writing with an audience.* Written form is only one of the ways to publish your writing.

Prewriting

How to Get an Idea

Some writers think this is the most difficult stage in the writing process. "What do I write about?" On the one hand, the possibilities are endless. On the other hand, that thought is not very comforting... or helpful. The task is to choose among all those possible topics and to do so wisely, carefully, and appropriately. But how?

1. Ideas for writing can come from many places and in many ways. First, look around you. The old saying "Write about what you know" has some truth in it. Ideas for writing can come from the everyday experiences you have with family and friends, with people you meet, with activities you do, with events and places you see. Make a list of favorite people, places, and things. Think about your favorite hobbies, activities, or skills. What is something you know how to do well and could explain to others? Have you recently read a story, book, or poem that made an impression on you?

2. You can write about past experiences or memories. If you keep a journal, it can be a good source for memory ideas. Look through old photographs or talk to family members to see what kinds of memories you can recall.

3. Read newspapers and magazines. Listen to the radio and television. Pay attention to what is going on in your community, in your state, in the nation, and in the world.

4. Try writing down anything that comes to mind. No matter how silly or useless your writing may seem, keep putting the words on paper as they flow through your head. When you go back and read what you wrote, you may find an idea there.

5. Talk with others about your ideas. Just hearing yourself say your ideas out loud may help you decide whether they seem like good writing topics or not. Try the ideas out on classmates, friends, or family members. They may be able to offer suggestions.

6. You might be able to use a graphic aid or some kind of visual device to help you find a topic. Try drawing a picture, diagram, map, chart, or idea web.

You use an **idea web** to make connections between ideas. In the center of your paper, write a possible subject and circle it. Then write any related ideas around the center circle. Circle them and draw lines from those circles to the center circle. Continue to add as many circles and lines as you wish. Your idea web can help you identify writing topics related to your original subject that may be a more usable size. (Later, you can also use your web to think of details about your topic.)

You can make a list based on the same concept as the idea web. Write a possible subject; then list examples or details related to the subject. From that list, choose one item and make another list of details. Again, this process can not only help you find a writing topic in a broad subject, but also show you whether you have enough details to begin writing.

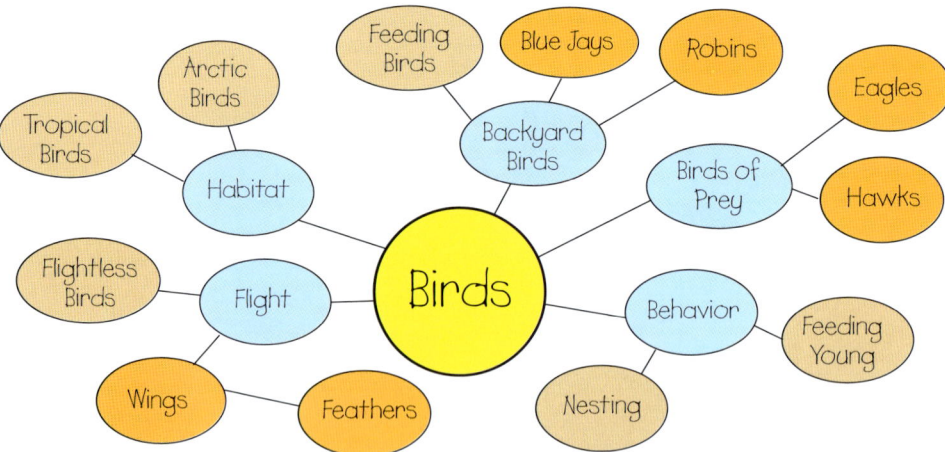

You can use a chart to think of ideas. Perhaps you are thinking about writing a description. Write a possible subject at the top of the chart; then make five columns, one for each sense. Write appropriate details in each column. Writing the details may give you an idea for a topic. Or, as with the idea web, the chart can be used to provide details for your later writing.

7. Ask yourself questions about a subject. See if you can get a personal angle on the subject by answering these questions: "Why do I want to write about this? What do I know about it? What do I want to know about it?"

Try asking *who, what, where, when, why,* and *how* questions about a subject. Questions, like graphic aids, can help you see the parts of a subject so that you can decide which part or parts you want to write about.

8. Whatever methods you use to generate ideas for topics, try to choose a topic that matters to you. The whole writing process will be much more interesting, exciting, and worthwhile if you choose something you care about or that interests you. It doesn't have to be something you like or enjoy; it could be something you dislike or that angers you.

Think of something you feel angry, sad, or joyful about. Think of an important or difficult problem or issue you have faced. Did you find a solution? If so, telling about the problem and solution might be helpful to others. The important thing is to be involved in the topic you write about.

9. Prepare for future writing by collecting ideas all the time. Save that list of favorite people, places, and things you made. Clip interesting newspaper and magazine articles. Jot down anything that might be of use later. Put these items in a notebook or folder to use the next time you need an idea for writing.

How to Develop a Topic

You have chosen your topic. Now what do you do? You start collecting lots of supporting details for your topic. There are different kinds of supporting details. The ones you use depend on what you are writing.

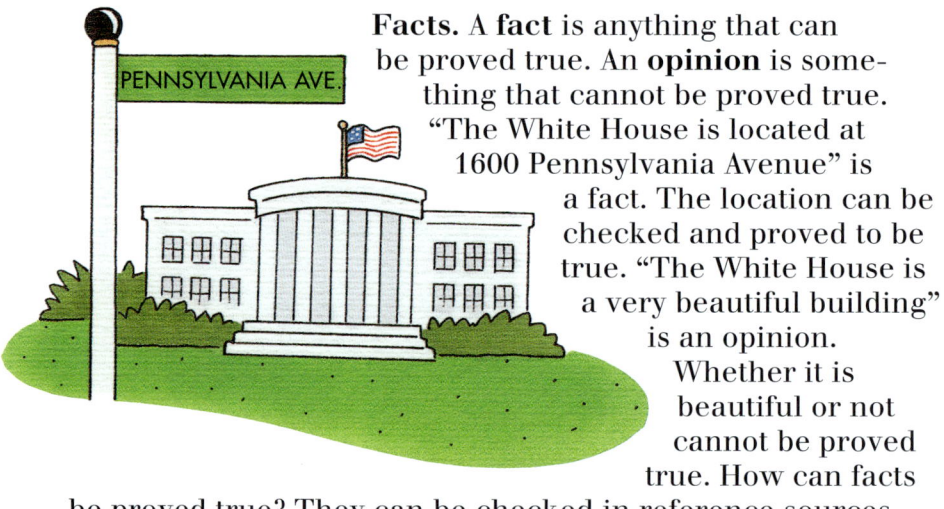

Facts. A **fact** is anything that can be proved true. An **opinion** is something that cannot be proved true. "The White House is located at 1600 Pennsylvania Avenue" is a fact. The location can be checked and proved to be true. "The White House is a very beautiful building" is an opinion. Whether it is beautiful or not cannot be proved true. How can facts be proved true? They can be checked in reference sources, such as encyclopedias. When you write, you use facts to support your main idea.

Reasons. These are logical explanations or arguments that you use to support your opinion. For example, if you think a historic building should be saved, you might explain how the building could be used, argue the importance of keeping some things from the past, and point out the value of the building as a tourist attraction.

Examples. These are instances of something that you use to support a point. For example, in your campaign to save the historic building, you might offer examples of historic buildings saved in other cities and how they proved to be beneficial to the cities.

Sensory details. These tell how things look, taste, feel, smell, and sound. They are most often used in descriptions. For example, in a description of an old building, you might describe how the rooms look and smell, how the floors creak, and how the woodwork feels.

Stories or events. You can tell a particular story or describe a particular event to support a point. The story or event may be from your own or others' experiences. It may be from your reading or your imagination. For example, in your campaign to save the historic building, you might tell the story of the building's architect or describe a president's historic visit to the building.

Where do all these details come from? First, look back at the prewriting you did when you were exploring your topic. In your notes, lists, charts, and webs, you will probably find many details.

But what if you still do not have enough details? How do you get more details? Here are some suggestions:

Research. Go to the library. Look in books, magazines, encyclopedias, and other reference sources. For much of the writing you do, research will be your primary source of details.

Interview. Get information from other people. For a description of a party, this might be some of the people who attended the party. For a report on snakes, this might be the keeper at the zoo's reptile house and a herpetologist (a person who studies reptiles and amphibians).

Observe. Look at things closely and describe them carefully. How does a snake move?

Remember. Think about what you can recall from your own experience. Have you ever encountered any snakes?

Imagine. Use your imagination. What do you think it would be like to be a snake?

The details you find may make you want to change your topic. You may find something that you think would be even more interesting to write about than your first topic idea. Such adjustments are a natural part of the writing process, especially during the prewriting stage. Go ahead and change your idea; then begin a new list of details.

Reason for Writing and Audience

An important part of prewriting is answering these two questions:

- Why am I writing?
- For whom am I writing?

The answers to these questions will have a major impact on your writing. Why? Read on to find out.

Why Am I Writing?

When you write, you must have a reason for writing. Common reasons for writing are to entertain, to inform, to persuade, and to express oneself. Each time you write, you need to ask yourself: Why am I writing this?

Of course, your reason for writing might be "Because I have to," but while that *is* a reason, it is not a reason that will help you very much. Knowing your goals for your writing will help you focus your writing.

For example, you are writing an account of a visit to the beach. Do you want to entertain your audience? If so, then you might focus on the amusing things that happened or the interesting people you met. Do you want to inform your audience? If so, then you might focus on facts about the beach.

You can have more than one reason for writing. Perhaps you wish to entertain *and* inform your audience about the beach. You might blend amusing incidents with informative facts. Whatever reason you choose, it's important to have one.

You may know your reasons before you begin writing. You may figure them out as you write. As with other parts of your writing, you may revise your reasons as you work.

For Whom Am I Writing?

You answer this question by identifying your audience, the people you are writing for. For a school writing assignment, your audience will probably be your teacher and perhaps your classmates. For a letter, your audience will be whomever the letter is addressed to. For a journal, your audience will be you. In each case, thinking about your audience helps you decide what to say.

Each time you write, ask yourself:

- What does my audience know?
- What might they want to know?
- What do I want to tell them?

The answers to these questions will help you decide what information you want to include or exclude when you write.

Your audience can also influence your level of language. In some situations, you would use more formal language. Imagine writing a letter to the editor of a newspaper or an article for a magazine. In other situations, such as a letter to a relative or a story for a friend, you would use more informal language.

Consider how writing for young children might be different from writing for adults. For young children, you might write about only one main idea with a few details. You would use short sentences, easy words, and very informal language. For adults, you might write about several main ideas with many details. You would use longer, more complex sentences, difficult words, and more formal language.

Drafting

Getting Organized

You have chosen your topic, chosen some details, considered your reasons for writing, and thought about your audience. You have a lot of ideas. Now what? It is time to write your first draft.

Drafting is putting your ideas down on paper. There are many different ways to draft, probably as many ways as there are writers. With practice, you will find out what kind of drafting works best for you.

Some writers like to sketch out a plan before they begin writing. They might make a list of ideas in a particular order or an outline that lists major topics and their subtopics. Then they write a draft following the list or outline. Some writers like to just write down their ideas as the ideas come to them and then rearrange, add, or delete ideas afterward.

A draft is only a first writing. You have to read the draft and decide what to keep and what to change. Then you write a second draft that reflects those changes. You might write several drafts before you have one you consider final. Also, drafting may send you back to prewriting to look for more ideas or details or even to reconsider your topic. Then you would write another draft.

Remember, the purpose of drafting is to get going on the writing. Do not stop to struggle with writing the perfect beginning sentence. That can come later.

Here are some ways to organize your details:

- Details can be organized around a main idea. Write a sentence that tells your main idea and then write all the details (facts, reasons, examples) that support that idea. This kind of organization is often used in persuasive or informative writing.

- Details can be organized in chronological order, or the order in which events happen. Often, signal words, such as *first, next, last,* and *finally,* are used to indicate the sequence of events. Chronological order is often used in stories, directions, and science or history reports.

- Details can be organized by order of importance. The writer gives the most important detail first, then the next most important detail, and so on down to the least important detail. This kind of organization may be used in persuasive or informative writing.

- Details can be organized by the way they are arranged in space. The writer begins at one place and then moves on, left to right, top to bottom, room by room, and so on. Details in descriptive writing are often organized in this way.

Different kinds of writing work best with different kinds of organization. Also, more than one kind of organization can be used in one piece of writing.

Try to write your whole draft at one time. Include everything you can think of. You can always make decisions later about what to keep and what to take out. No matter how clumsy and rough you may think your first draft is, remember you must have a draft in order to have something to work with. Also, by writing, you will clarify your thoughts. You will see what you have and what you need to get.

It is a good idea to put a first draft aside before reading it. Time can make some things clearer. Also, you may wish to get others people's comments and ideas about your writing. Ask someone to read one of your drafts. See pages 110–111 for advice on evaluating your own work and having others evaluate it.

Writing Paragraphs

What is a **paragraph?** You may think of a paragraph as a group of sentences, and so it is. But there is more to a paragraph than that. First, the sentences that make up a paragraph must work together to state and develop the same main idea. Second, the sentences in a paragraph must be arranged in an order that makes sense. Third, a paragraph may contain a topic sentence.

What is a **topic sentence?** It states the main idea of the paragraph. Often a topic sentence is at or near the beginning of a paragraph. A paragraph does not *have* to have a topic sentence, but it is not a bad idea to write one for each paragraph whether you use it or not. The topic sentence can help make the main idea of the paragraph clear to you. And that can help you when you are adding or deleting details in the paragraph.

Another way to focus on the main idea of a paragraph is to write down everything you can think of when you are writing the first draft of the paragraph. Then think about the main idea, or the message you are trying to get across. Take out any details that are not related to that main idea. Add details that help develop that main idea.

What makes a good paragraph? In a good paragraph, all the sentences stay focused on the paragraph's main idea. They explain and support the main idea by giving details such as facts, incidents, examples, and reasons. (See pages 100–101 about gathering details to develop a topic.) The sentences also give all the information that readers need to understand the main idea. Moreover, all the sentences are clearly and logically related to each other. They are arranged in an order that readers will have no trouble following and understanding. Just as bricks should fit together well to make a solid wall, sentences should fit together well to make a good paragraph.

One way to help readers is to use transitions that make links between the details in the sentences. Transitions may indicate time (*first, last, today, yesterday, now, then*); they may indicate an arrangement in space (*above, below, inside, outside*); they may indicate order of importance (*first, second, third*); they may indicate a comparison or contrast (*as, like, both, but, yet, however*). These words act as clues for readers, alerting them to relationships between the ideas.

How can you revise a paragraph to make it better?

• Identify the main idea. If you can't identify it, your readers won't be able to, either. Perhaps you need to add a topic sentence stating the main idea.

• Make sure all the details develop the main idea. Delete any details that are unrelated to the main idea.

• Make sure you have included enough details. Does your paragraph raise more questions than it answers? If so, maybe you need to add more information.

• Make sure the order of the sentences makes sense. Perhaps you need to rearrange the sentences or add some transitions to them.

In a way, writing a good paragraph is a lot like writing a whole story or report. A story or report introduces, develops, and concludes a main idea. Its paragraphs are arranged in a sensible order that readers can easily follow. Its subject is fully and carefully explained. So is it with a good paragraph. A paragraph has a main idea that it introduces (often in a topic sentence), develops (using relevant details), and concludes. The sentences in a paragraph are arranged logically and clearly. And the paragraph contains all the details needed to explain the main idea. So once you know the basics of writing a good paragraph, you know the basics of writing a good story or report.

How to Begin

The introduction to your writing is important. It may be several paragraphs or just one sentence. However long it is, it must tell readers what they will be reading about and it must catch a reader's interest and attention.

It might seem logical to simply announce what you are writing about. For example, "This story is about..." or "My subject is...". For most kinds of writing, such a blunt announcement is just not interesting enough to be a good introduction.

Here are some suggestions for introductions:

• **Begin with a story.** A very short story, or anecdote, especially a humorous one, can be a good way to begin. But remember, the story is intended only to lead to your main topic.

• **Begin with a fact.** You can begin with an interesting or unusual bit of information, something that will immediately attract a reader.

• **Begin with a question.** Asking a question can make a reader read to find the answer. Asking a question addressed to the reader can help involve the reader in the subject right from the start.

• **Begin with a quotation.** Sometimes a piece of writing will begin with a quotation by an expert on the topic or by a famous person.

One of the best ways to improve your own introductions is to pay close attention to the introductions of the stories and articles you read. See what other writers do to try to grab a reader's attention. Then the next time you write, try an introduction like one of those you admired.

How to End

As with the introduction, the conclusion to your writing is important. It may be a single sentence or a paragraph. Whatever its length, the conclusion must tell your reader clearly and strongly "The End," but without actually using those words!

Worse than actually saying "The End" is having no ending at all, just a kind of trailing off that leaves your reader dissatisfied or confused. You may have a terrific introduction and wonderful ideas expressed in solid paragraphs and then ruin the whole thing with a weak conclusion.

In general, the conclusion is your last chance to get across to the reader whatever it is you have been trying to say in the rest of your writing. A conclusion is not the place to introduce anything new; it is the place to look back at what has gone before.

Here are some suggestions for conclusions:

• **End with a summary.** Most nonfiction writing ends with a review or summary of what was presented in the body of the writing. This approach is helpful because it leaves the reader with a clear restatement of the main idea.

• **End with a suggestion.** In persuasive writing, a writer may end by offering a suggestion of something that the reader should think or do. This suggestion is usually related to whatever opinion the writer is expressing in the piece.

• **End with the last event.** Usually, in stories or any kind of writing with a chronological order, whatever happens last in the story or sequence of events is the ending. This happened first, this second, and this last.

As you did with introductions, you should study the conclusions of stories and articles you read to see how other writers end their writing. Which conclusions do you think work and which ones do not? Why? Then, the next time you write, try using one of the conclusions you liked as a guide.

Revising

You have written your first draft. Now what? It is time to revise.

The goal of revising is to improve what you have written. The process of revising involves looking at your work, seeing what you like and do not like, and deciding what you want to change and how you will change it.

Revising may mean doing more than just adding a word here or taking out a word there. You may decide to rearrange paragraphs, reword a section, or add sentences. You may do a little revising; you may do a lot. You may even decide to start over and write a whole new draft!

Like prewriting and drafting, revising can take place at any time. You are revising as you organize the information about your topic. You are revising as you reorganize the information while you are writing a draft. Moreover, revising can take place many times during the course of completing a piece of writing.

After you have completed a draft, set it aside for a while. Then take it out and read it. By letting some time pass, you will be able to see things in your writing more clearly, which will help you revise.

Read your draft aloud. Hearing the words can help you evaluate your writing. Awkward words or sentences will stand out more. Gaps in your reasoning or arguments will show up more.

Ask yourself questions about your draft:

- Does my introduction catch a reader's attention?
- Is my main idea clear?
- Is my main idea supported by enough details?
- Do all the details relate to the main idea?
- Should any of the details be taken out?
- Do I need to add any paragraph breaks?
- Is my material organized clearly and logically?
- Is there anything I can add that will make my writing more interesting?
- Does my conclusion clearly indicate "The End"?

Other people can give you advice about your writing. Read your draft to them, or let them read it. There is no better way to find out whether or not you got your message across clearly than to have another person read your writing.

Encourage your reader to offer specific comments and suggestions. A vague "very nice" comment is not very helpful to you. You need to know what was good (and bad) and why. If necessary, ask your reader questions such as these:

- Did anything in my writing confuse you?
- What did you like best or find most interesting?
- What do you think is my main idea?
- Did I answer any questions you might have about my topic?

Listen carefully to what your reader has to say. Do not take the comments too personally; remember, you asked for the person's advice. And after all, you do not have to follow this advice if you do not want to.

Use both your own evaluation and the comments of others to figure out what works and what does not work in your writing. Then you can revise to eliminate problems.

Proofreading

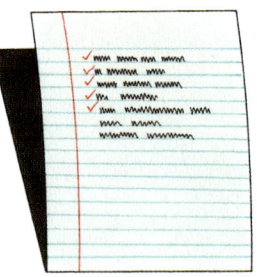

Once you think you have finished any major revisions to your writing, proofread your work. You show respect for yourself and your reader when you make your writing as readable as possible. Now is the time to look for and correct mistakes in spelling, grammar, punctuation, and capitalization. Such things may seem minor, especially when compared to larger issues such as good organization of ideas, solid topic sentences, and sufficient detail. But mechanical errors can distract and confuse a reader. You want the reader to pay attention to your writing and your ideas, *not* your mistakes.

Here are some strategies you can use when you proofread:

• Proofread slowly and carefully. You might make a checklist of questions. (See the example below.) The questions should reflect any particular areas in which you have had difficulty before.

Spelling

☐ Have I spelled all the words correctly?

(If you keep a list of problem words as suggested on page 118, use the word list as part of your checklist.)

Grammar

☐ Have I written complete sentences?

☐ Have I used the correct verb forms?

☐ Do the subjects and verbs agree?

(See pages 6–70 for information on grammar.)

Capitalization

☐ Have I capitalized the first words of sentences?

☐ Have I capitalized proper nouns?

(See pages 72–78 for information on capitalization.)

Punctuation

☐ Have I used an end mark after every sentence?

☐ Have I used commas correctly?

(See pages 79–94 for information on punctuation.)

The Writing Process • 113

• Set your work aside and come back to proofread it later. It will be easier to see your mistakes then.

• Proofread aloud. This can be helpful in checking for complete sentences, end punctuation, and commas in sentences.

• Proofread more than once. Look for different things each time. You might check for grammar errors in one reading, capitalization errors in a second reading, and so on.

• Proofread with a dictionary and a grammar handbook nearby. You can use these sources to check any questions you might have. As you read, mark the places where you have questions, finish reading, and then answer the questions.

• Use a computer spell checker, but do not rely on it alone. A computer spell checker will catch some spelling errors, but it cannot help when you write *there* instead of *their* or *student* when you meant *students.* You must proofread your writing yourself to find those kinds of mistakes.

• Ask someone else to proofread your work. This can be helpful, of course, but it is still best to proofread your own work at least once.

114 • The Writing Process

You can help make your proofreading faster and more efficient by using proofreading marks. Put the appropriate mark at the place where you mean to make the change.

Here are some common proofreading marks followed by an example of how to use the marks when proofreading a paragraph.

Proofreading Marks

≡ Capitalize the letter.
/ Make the capital letter lowercase.
⊙ Add a period.
⌃̦ Add a comma.
∧ Add the letter(s) or word(s).
⌿ Take out the letter(s) or word(s).
⌒ Close up the space.
¶ Begin a new paragraph.
∽ Reverse the position of the letters or words.

The English /Writer Arthur ≡conan Doyle created the fict⌒oi̯nal

detective Sherlock Holmes. Holmes∧^first appeared in the story "A

Study in Scarlet" in 1887⊙Tired of writing stor∽ies about Holmes⌃̦

Doyle tried∧to kill off the chara∧cter in 1893, but an out⌿raged

public forced ⌿him Doyle to bring Holmes back.

Publishing

You probably think of publishing as getting your writing published in a newspaper or magazine or as a book. Think of publishing instead as any way you can present and share your writing with an audience, which includes getting it printed.

The following publishing ideas are suitable for all kinds of writing:

- Produce a classroom newspaper or magazine several times a year or once a month. The newspaper or magazine will feature writing by you and your classmates. Share this newspaper or magazine with students in other classes or with family members at home.

- Submit your writing to the school newspaper or to a local or community newspaper or magazine.

- Get together with others and take turns reading your work aloud. Discuss each other's writing afterward.

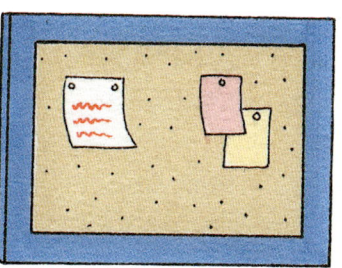

- Post your writing on the class bulletin board for all to read.

- Give your writing as an oral presentation.

- Make copies of your writing to share with anyone who is interested, including friends and family members.

Some publishing ideas, such as the following, are more suitable for certain kinds of writing:

- Mail a letter to the person it is intended for.

- Make a persuasive essay or opinion piece into a letter to the editor and submit it to a newspaper.
- Make a persuasive essay or opinion piece into a poster and arrange to hang it in the lunchroom or a hallway.
- Use a persuasive essay or opinion piece as part of a debate.
- Submit book, movie, or music reviews to the school newspaper.
- Read a story aloud to younger students or family members.
- Turn a story into a skit or play for younger students or family members.

- Read aloud and perform a demonstration with a report that explains a process.

Completing the Writing Process

One part of completing the writing process is finding a way to share your final product with an audience. Thinking about your writing is also part of completing the writing process.

To gain from your writing experience, think about these questions:

- What did you do this time that you would do the same the next time you write?
- What did you do this time that you would do differently?
- Which parts did you like?
- Which parts did you have trouble with?

You might write the answers to these questions. When you save your writing, save the answers to the questions, too. Start a writing portfolio in a notebook or a folder. Keep your writing, your answers, and your writing ideas in your portfolio.

Skills for Writing

Using a Dictionary

A **dictionary** is a special kind of reference book that lists words, their spellings, and their definitions. A dictionary also gives other information about words. Knowing how a dictionary is organized can help you when you need to use this important book.

1. The words listed in a dictionary are called **entry words.** The entry words are listed in alphabetical order, that is, the order of the letters in the alphabet, A to Z.

2. At the top of every page of a dictionary are two words called **guide words.** You can use guide words to find the page that has the word you are looking for. The guide word on the left is the first entry word on a page. The guide word on the right is the last entry word on the page. If your word comes alphabetically between the two guide words on a page, then it will appear on that page.

3. The **dictionary entry** is the information about an entry word. First, the entry word is shown divided into syllables. Next is the **pronunciation guide,** which is the entry word spelled using symbols that stand for sounds. (The **pronunciation key,** found at the bottom of the right-hand pages or at the front of the dictionary, explains the symbols.) Next, the entry gives the word's **part of speech** using an abbreviation such as *n.* or *adj.* This is followed by the **definition,** which tells the meaning of the word. An entry may also include the word's **history**—where it came from and how it developed—and **synonyms** for the word. A synonym is another word with the same or a similar meaning.

Different dictionaries may organize the information in their entries in different ways. Some may include information that others do not. Usually, a dictionary has an introduction that explains how the dictionary is organized.

Spelling Help

Here are some things you can do to help yourself become a better speller:

1. When you first see a new word, look at it closely. Pronounce the word carefully, emphasizing each syllable. Then look at each letter. (Many common spelling errors result from leaving out letters or syllables.) Picture the complete word in your mind. Write the word. Check to see that you have spelled it correctly.

2. Keep a list of problem words. Make a list of any words that you have had trouble spelling, particularly any words that you have misspelled more than once. Use the list as your personal reference source.

3. Use a dictionary. Look up a word whenever you are not absolutely certain of its spelling. (Even if you are certain, it can't hurt to double-check!)

4. Proofread your writing. Careful proofreading can help you find many common errors, including misspelled words.

5. Create **mnemonics,** or memory devices. A mnemonic is anything that helps you remember how a particular word is spelled. For example, the singing rhyme for spelling *Mississippi (M-i-s-s, i-s-s, i-p-p-i, it used to be so hard to spell...)* is a mnemonic. To remember that *necessary* has one *c* and two *s*'s, you might make up a sentence such as *It is necessary to call Susie and Sam.* To remember that *accommodate* has two *c*'s and two *m*'s, you might make a picture in your mind of **two c**ats chasing **two m**ice. Think about creating mnemonics for problem words on your list. Mnemonics are best for the words you have trouble spelling. You might not want to try them for every new word you learn.

6. Remember a few spelling rules.

- Is it *ie* or *ei?* Use *ie* when the letters spell the long *e* sound, except after *c.*

    bel**ie**ve   p**ie**ce   f**ie**ld
    ceiling   re**cei**ve   de**cei**ve

Exceptions to this rule:

    seize   leisure
    either   neither

- When a prefix is added to a word, the spelling of the word does not change.

    un + likely = **un**likely   mis + spell = **mis**spell
    dis + agree = **dis**agree   re + view = **re**view

- For most words with a final *e*, drop the *e* before adding a suffix that begins with a vowel. Keep the *e* before adding a suffix that begins with a consonant.

    writ**e** + ing = writing   mov**e** + ed = moved
    hop**e** + less = hop**e**less   car**e** + ful = car**e**ful

- For words ending in a consonant and a *y*, change the *y* to *i* before adding a suffix that does *not* begin with *i*.

    hurry + ed = hurr**i**ed   pity + ful = pit**i**ful
    hurry + ing = hurr**y**ing   pity + ing = pit**y**ing

- Double the final consonant before adding a suffix that begins with a vowel if

(a) the word has one syllable and ends with one consonant preceded by one vowel.

    run + ing = run**n**ing
    hot + est = hot**t**est

(b) the word has more than one syllable, ends with one consonant preceded by one vowel, and is accented on the last syllable.

    admit + ed = admit**t**ed
    forget + ing = forget**t**ing
    offer + ed = offered
    profit + ing = profiting
    (*Offer* and *profit* are accented on the first syllable.)

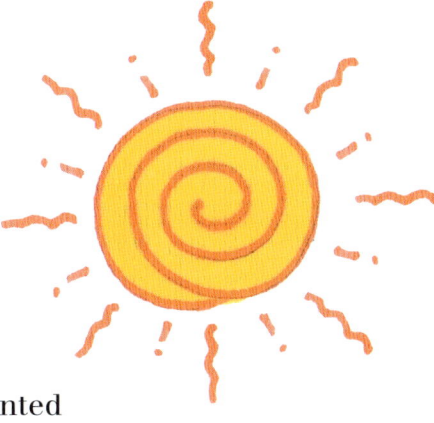

Using a Thesaurus

A **thesaurus** is a special kind of reference book that contains synonyms and antonyms for words. **Synonyms** are words that have the same or similar meanings. *Cold* and *cool* are synonyms because they have similar meanings. **Antonyms** are words that have opposite meanings. *Cold* and *hot* are antonyms because they have opposite meanings.

You can use a thesaurus to make your writing more specific. It can help you find words that have exactly the meaning you want. You can also use a thesaurus to make your writing more interesting or exciting. It can help you find many different words to express the same meaning.

Some thesauruses are arranged alphabetically. If you looked up the word *say* in one of these thesauruses, you might see an entry like this one:

> **say,** *v.* **1.** speak, remark, pronounce, utter, affirm, allege **2.** tell, state, declare, express, argue, word **3.** recite, repeat, reiterate, rehearse **4.** report, allege, maintain, hold

Some thesauruses are arranged with an index at the back. If you looked up the word *say* in one of these thesauruses, you might see a list like this one in the index:

> **say**
> *affirm* 532 vb.
> *speak* 579 vb.

Then if you turned to section 579, you might see a list like this:

> **Vb.** *speak,* mention, say; utter, articulate 577 vb. *voice,* pronounce, declare 524 vb. *hint,* talk 570 vb. *recite,* read, dictate

Any of the words in either entry might be good ones to use in place of *say,* but it is important to remember that synonyms do have slightly different meanings. It is a good idea to check the meaning of a synonym in a dictionary before using it in a sentence.

recite   tell   DECLARE   express   report

Choosing the Right Word

Here are some commonly misused and misspelled words. Writers often have problems with these words because they sound alike or very similar. Use the meanings and example sentences to help you choose the right word to use.

Accept-Except

Accept is a verb meaning "to receive" or "to agree to." *Except* is most often used as a preposition meaning "not including." But *except* can also be used as a verb meaning "to leave out."

> I **accept** your invitation to the party.
> Everyone **except** Jason will be coming. He will be **excepted** from attending.

Affect-Effect

Affect is most often used as a verb meaning "to influence." It is also sometimes used as a noun meaning "feelings" or "how a person appears to feel." *Effect* is most often used as a noun meaning "result of an action."

> The water pollution will **affect** the fish.
> The counselor observed the patient's **affect**.
> The **effect** of the water pollution is dead fish.

Council-Counsel

Council is a noun meaning "a group of people called together to discuss questions and give advice." *Counsel* as a noun means "advice." *Counsel* as a verb means "to give advice to."

> The town **council** discusses land development.
> Experts give them **counsel** on different issues.
> A professor **counsels** them on animal habitats.

Emigrate–Immigrate

Emigrate means "to go from a country" and settle somewhere else. *Immigrate* means "to come into a country" and settle there.

> In the 1850s, many people **emigrated** from Ireland.
> Many Irish **immigrated** to the United States.

Its–It's

Its is a possessive pronoun. It has no apostrophe. *It's* is a contraction for *it is*. The apostrophe replaces the missing letter *i*.

> **It's** time to take the dog for a walk.
> The dog carries **its** leash in **its** mouth.

Principal–Principle

Principal as an adjective means "most important." *Principal* as a noun means "head of a school." *Principle* means "general truth" or "rule of conduct."

> Ms. Javier is the **principal** of our school.
> Her **principal** task is to keep the school running.
> She believes in the **principle** of fairness.

Their–There–They're

Their is a pronoun meaning "belonging to them." It is the possessive form of *they*. *There* is usually an adverb meaning "in or to that place." *They're* is a contraction for *they are*.

> **Their** car broke down on the way to the airport.
> They were supposed to be **there** by 5:00 P.M.
> **They're** going to be late meeting the plane.

To-Too-Two

To is usually a preposition meaning "toward" or "in the direction of." *Too* is an adverb meaning "also" or "very." *Two* is the word for the number 2.

> **Too** many birds came **to** the bird feeder.
> A cardinal and a blue jay are waiting, **too.**
> There isn't room for **two** more.

Whose-Who's

Whose is the possessive form of the pronoun *who*. It has no apostrophe. *Who's* is a contraction for *who is* or *who has*. The apostrophe replaces the missing letter or letters.

> **Whose** turn is it to pick up the pizza?
> Do you know **who's** going to pick up the pizza?

Your-You're

Your is the possessive form of the pronoun *you*. It has no apostrophe. *You're* is a contraction for *you are*. The apostrophe replaces the missing letter *a*.

> **Your** sister is looking for you.
> She says **you're** supposed to go home now.

See pages 34–35 for information on using confusing verbs and page 64–65 for information on using confusing prepositions.

Index

A
abbreviations, 73, 79–80, 89
accept, vs. except, 121
action verbs, 11, 23, 25, 41
addresses, punctuation of, 86
adjective phrases, 62
adjectives, 47–53
   adverbs vs., 55–56
   articles, 49
   clauses as, 45
   commas with, 84
   common, 48
   comparisons with, 52–53
   defined, 47, 55
   demonstrative, 50
   as interjections, 68
   possessives as, 42, 48, 50
   predicate, 26, 51
   prepositional phrases as, 62
   pronouns as, 42, 48, 50
   proper, 48, 72–75
   questions answered by, 47–48
adverb phrases, 62
adverbs, 54–59, 62, 64, 68
affect, vs. effect, 121
among, vs. between, 65
antecedents, 36–37, 45
antonyms, 120
apostrophe, 20, 21–22, 42, 90–91
appositives, 83
articles, 49
audience, for writing, 103

B
bad, vs. badly, 56
beside, vs. besides, 65
between, vs. among, 65
bring, vs. take, 34

C
can, vs. may, 34
capitalization, 72–78
   abbreviations, 73, 89
   outlines, 77
   poems, 77
   pronouns, 73
   proofreading checklist, 112
   proper adjectives, 48, 72–75
   proper nouns, 17, 72–75, 78
   quotations, 76
   sentences, 76
   titles of works, 78
case, 38
clauses, 45, 67
colon, 88, 89
comma, 82–87
   in addresses, 86
   with adjectives, 84
   with appositives, 83
   in compound predicates, 13
   in compound sentences, 85
   in compound subjects, 12
   in dates, 86
   in direct address, 82
   with interjections, 68
   with interrupters, 83
   with introductory words, 82
   in letters, 87
   with quotation marks, 87, 93, 94
   in sentences, 12, 13, 82–85
   in a series, 84, 88
   with titles of works, 94
common adjectives, 48
common nouns, 17
comparative form, 52–53, 57–58
complete predicate, 10

complete subject, 10
compound objects, 41, 66
compound predicates (verbs), 13, 30, 66
compound sentences, 66, 85, 88
compound subjects, 12, 39–40, 66, 69
compound words, 20, 91
conclusion, in written works, 109
conjunctions, 12, 13, 66–67, 69, 85
contractions, 42, 90
council, vs. counsel, 121

D
dates, punctuation of, 86
declarative sentences, 14, 15, 79
demonstrative adjectives, 50
demonstrative pronouns, 44
dependent clauses, 67
dictionaries, 117, 118
dictionary entry, 117
direct address, 82
direct objects, 25
direct quotations, 76, 87, 92, 93
divided quotations, 76, 87, 93
double negatives, 59
drafting, 96, 104–109

E
effect, vs. affect, 121
emigrate, vs. immigrate, 122
entry words, 117
except, vs. accept, 121
exclamation point, 81
  with exclamatory sentences, 14, 68, 81
  with imperative sentences, 79, 81
  with interjections, 68, 81
  with quotation marks, 93, 94
exclamatory sentences, 14, 15, 68, 81

F
facts, defined, 100
first person pronouns, 38
fragments, sentence, 9
future perfect tense, 31
future tense, 30, 31

G
geographical names, 74, 78
good, vs. well, 56
grammar, 6–70
guide words, 117

H
helping verbs, 24, 32
hyphen, 91

I
ideas, how to get, 97–99
idea web, 98
immigrate, vs. emigrate, 122
imperative sentences, 14, 15, 79, 81
in, vs. into, 65
indefinite pronouns, 43, 46
indirect quotations, 92
initials, 72, 80
interjections, 68, 81
interrogative pronouns, 45
interrogative sentences, 14, 15, 45, 81
interrupters, 83
into, vs. in, 65
introduction, in written works, 108
irregular verbs, 30, 32–33
italics, 94
its, vs. it's, 122

L
lay, vs. lie, 35
lead, vs. led, 34
learn, vs. teach, 35
leave, vs. let, 34

led, vs. lead, 34
let, vs. leave, 34
letters, punctuation in, 87, 89
lie, vs. lay, 35
linking (state-of-being) verbs, 11, 23
　predicate words after, 26, 51
　pronouns with, 39, 40
lists, punctuation of, 80, 89

M
main clauses, 67
main verbs, 24
may, vs. can, 34
mechanics, 71–94
mnemonics, 118

N
names, proper, 17, 48, 72–75, 78
negatives, double, 59
nominative case, 38
nouns, 16–22. *See also* plural nouns; pronouns; singular nouns.
　common, 17
　defined, 16
　as objects, 25, 40–41, 60
　possessive, 21–22, 50, 90
　as predicate words, 26
　proper, 17, 72–75, 78
numbers, 77, 80

O
objective case, 38
objects
　compound, 41, 66
　direct, 25
　of prepositions, 40, 41, 60, 61, 63, 69
　of verbs, 25, 40–41, 63
outlines, 77, 80

P
paragraphs, writing of, 106–107
part of speech. *See also* specific parts of speech.
　determined by position in sentence, 70
　given in dictionary, 117

past part, of verb, 31, 33
past participles, 31, 32, 33
past perfect tense, 31
past tense, 29–30, 32
period, 79–80
　with abbreviations, 73, 79–80
　with declarative sentences, 14, 79
　with imperative sentences, 14, 79
　with initials, 72, 80
　with interjections, 68
　in lists, 80
　with quotation marks, 93, 94
　with titles of works, 94
person, referred to by pronouns, 37, 38
personal names, 17, 72–73, 78
personal pronouns, 38
plural nouns, 18–20
　adjectives with, 49, 50
　agreement with verbs, 27–28, 46, 69
　possessive form of, 22, 90
　pronouns, 37, 38, 43, 46
　punctuation of, 20, 90
plural verbs, 27–28, 46, 69
poems, capitalization in, 77
possessive case, 21–22, 50, 90
　contractions vs., 42
　defined, 38
　of plurals, 22, 90
　of pronouns, 38, 42, 48, 50
　punctuation, 21–22, 42, 90
predicate adjectives, 26, 51
predicates, 8, 10, 11. *See also* verbs.
　compound, 13, 30, 66
　simple, 11
predicate words, 26, 51
prefixes, 119
prepositional phrases, 61, 62, 69
prepositions, 60–65
　objects of, 40, 41, 60, 61, 63, 69
present part, of verb, 31, 33
present perfect tense, 31
present tense, 29, 31
prewriting, 96, 97–103

principal, vs. principle, 122
pronouns, 36–46
  as adjectives, 42, 48, 50
  agreement with antecedents, 37
  agreement with verbs, 46
  antecedents of, 36–37, 45
  capitalization of, 73
  case, 38
  defined, 36
  demonstrative, 44
  indefinite, 43, 46
  interrogative, 45
  as objects, 40–41, 60, 63
  personal, 38
  plural/singular, 37, 38, 43, 46
  possessive, 38, 42, 48, 50
  as predicate words, 26
  relative, 45
  as subjects, 39–40
pronunciation guide, 117
pronunciation key, 117
proofreading, 96, 112–114
proper adjectives, 48, 72–75
proper nouns, 17, 72–75, 78
publishing, 96, 115–116
punctuation, 79–94. *See also* specific punctuation marks.
  abbreviations, 73, 79–80, 89
  addresses, 86
  adjectives, 84
  appositives, 83
  compound predicates, 13
  compound subjects, 12
  contractions, 90
  dates, 86
  direct address, 82
  initials, 72, 80
  interjections, 68, 81
  interrupters, 83
  introductory words, 82
  letters, 87, 89
  lists, 80, 89
  numbers, 80
  outlines, 80
  plurals, 20, 90
  possessives, 21–22, 42, 90
  proofreading checklist, 112

punctuation *(continued)*
  quotations, 87, 92–93
  sentences, 12–14, 68, 79, 81–85, 88, 94
  series, 84, 88
  times, 89
  titles of works, 94

Q

question mark, 14, 68, 81, 93, 94
quotation marks, 87, 92–93, 94
quotations, 76, 87, 92–93, 108

R

raise, vs. rise, 35
regular verbs, 30, 31, 32
relative pronouns, 45
revising, 96, 107, 110–111
rise, vs. raise, 35
run-on sentences, 9

S

second person pronouns, 38
semicolon, 88, 94
sentence fragments, 9
sentences, 7–15
  capitalization of, 76
  compound, 66, 85, 88
  declarative, 14, 15, 79
  defined, 7
  double negatives in, 59
  exclamatory, 14, 15, 68, 81
  fragments, 9
  imperative, 14, 15, 79, 81
  interrogative, 14, 15, 45, 81
  kinds of, 14
  predicates of. *See* predicates.
  punctuation of, 12–14, 68, 79, 81–85, 88, 94
  run-on, 9
  subjects of. *See* subjects.
  titles of works in, 94
  topic, 106
series, punctuation of, 84, 88
set, vs. sit, 35
simple predicate, 11. *See also* verbs.
simple subject, 10

singular nouns
  adjectives with, 49, 50
  agreement with verbs, 27–28, 46, 69
  defined, 18
  possessive form of, 22, 90
  pronouns, 37, 38, 43, 46
singular verbs, 27–28, 46, 69
sit, vs. set, 35
skills for writers, 117–123
speaker's tags, 87, 92, 93
spelling, 112, 113, 118–119, 121
state-of-being verbs. *See* linking (state-of-being) verbs.
subjects
  agreement with verbs, 27–28, 46, 69
  complete, 10
  compound, 12, 39–40, 66, 69
  defined, 8
  location in sentence, 15
  prepositional phrases in, 69
  pronouns as, 39–40
  simple, 10
  of specific types of sentences, 15
subject-verb agreement, 27–28, 46, 69
suffixes, 119
superlative form, 52–53, 57–58
synonyms, 117, 120

T
take, vs. bring, 34
teach, vs. learn, 35
tenses, verb, 29–30, 31, 32
their, vs. there, vs. they're, 122
thesauruses, 120
third person pronouns, 38
times, punctuation of, 89
titles, of persons, 72–73
titles, of works, 78, 94
to, vs. too, vs. two, 123

topics, writing
  development of, 100–101
  how to get ideas for, 97–99
topic sentences, 106

U
underlining, of titles, 94

V
verbs, 23–35. *See also* linking (state-of-being) verbs.
  action verbs, 11, 23, 25, 41
  agreement with nouns, 27–28, 46, 69
  commonly misused, 34–35
  defined, 23
  helping, 24, 32
  as interjections, 68
  irregular, 30, 32–33
  main, 24
  objects of, 25, 40–41, 63
  parts of, 31, 32–33
  regular, 30, 31, 32
  tenses of, 29–30, 31, 32

W
well, vs. good, 56
whose, vs. who's, 123
writing, 95–123
  audience for, 103
  conclusions, 109
  drafting, 96, 104–109
  ideas for, 97–99
  introductions, 108
  prewriting, 96, 97–103
  process, 96–116
  proofreading, 96, 112–114
  publishing, 96, 115–116
  reasons for, 102
  revising, 96, 107, 110–111
  topic development, 100–101

Y
your, vs. you're, 123

handy homework helper

How to Write School Reports

study reference guide

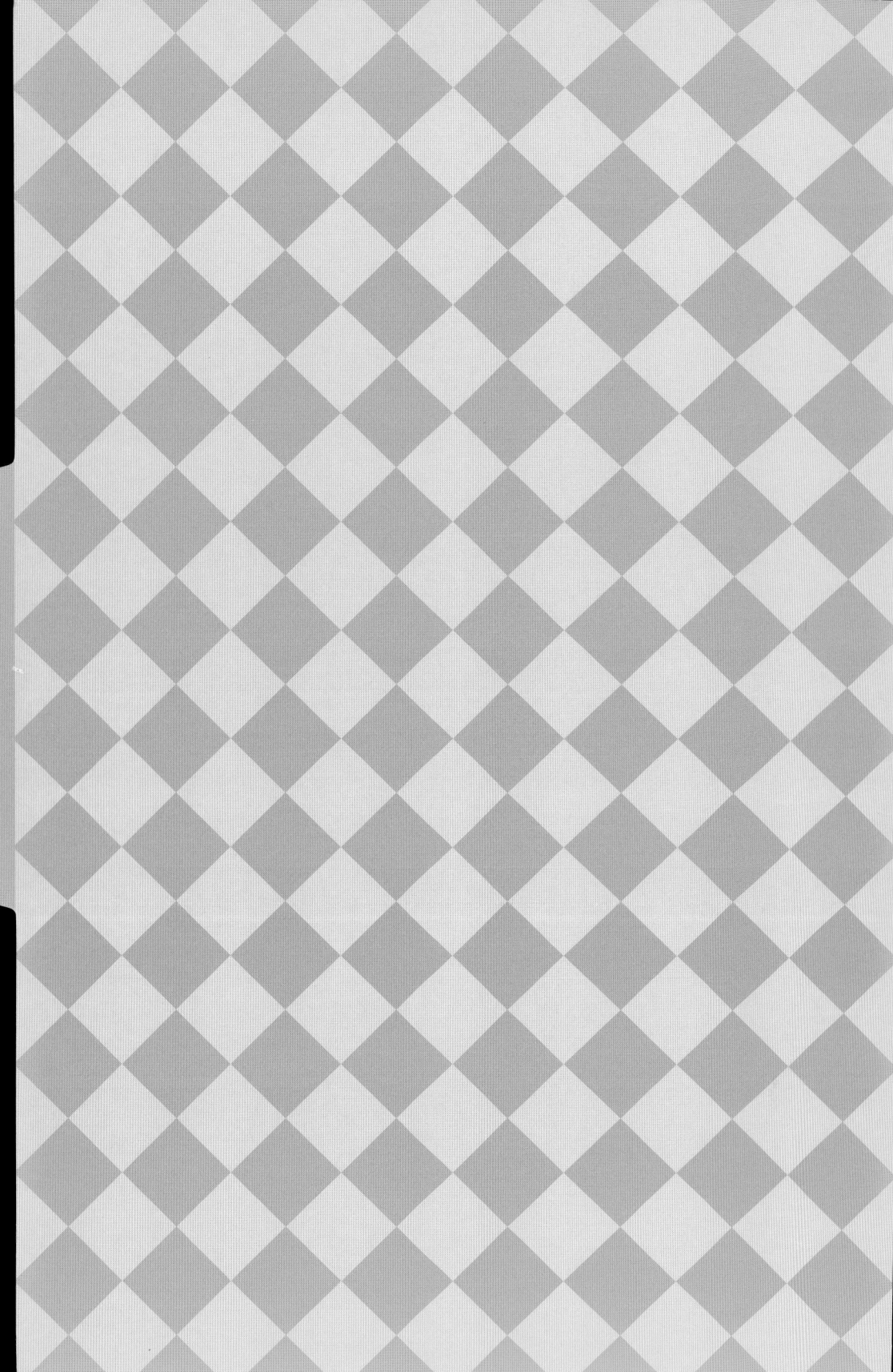

handy **homework** helper

How to Write School Reports

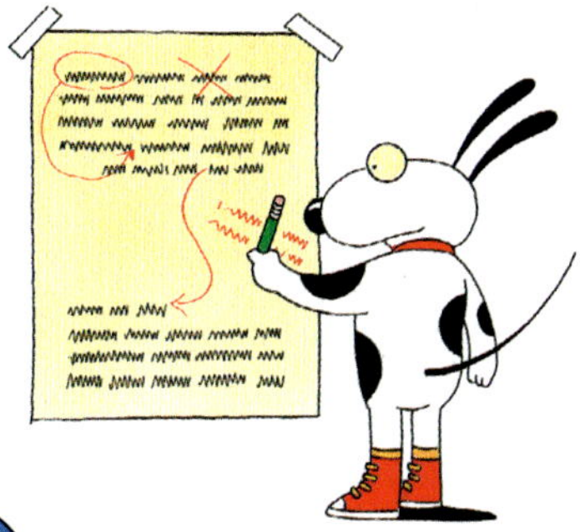

Writer:
Helen H. Moore

Consultant:
Carl B. Smith, Ph.D.

pil
Publications International, Ltd.

Helen H. Moore is a journalist, poet, and published author of educational and children's books. She has taught language arts for elementary school grades and served as an editor for a national educational publisher. Her work includes *A Poem a Day: 180 Thematic Poems and Activities That Teach and Delight All Year Long* and *The 100 Best Brain-Boosters: Puzzles and Games to Stimulate Students' Thinking*.

Carl B. Smith, Ph.D., is Professor Emeritus at Indiana University and directs the Education Resource Information Center (ERIC) for reading, English and communication, and the Family Literacy Center. In 1997 Dr. Smith received the Indiana Literacy Award for his many contributions to reading instruction across the country. He has authored more than 40 books for teachers and parents including *Help Your Child Read and Succeed* and *Improving Your Children's Composition*.

Illustrations: Chris Reed

Copyright © 2005 Publications International, Ltd. All rights reserved. This book may not be reproduced or quoted in whole or in part by any means whatsoever without written permission from:

Louis Weber, CEO
Publications International, Ltd.
7373 North Cicero Avenue
Lincolnwood, Illinois 60712

Permission is never granted for commercial purposes.

Manufactured in China.

8 7 6 5 4 3 2 1

ISBN: 0-7853-3490-4

Contents

About This Book • 4
1. Me? Write a Report? • 5
2. Generating Ideas • 11
3. Research • 21
4. Taking Notes • 30
5. Creating an Outline • 41
6. The Introduction and Rough Draft • 52
7. The Body of the Report • 65
8. The Conclusion • 69
9. Revision • 73
10. Editing and Proofreading • 78
11. Publishing • 96
12. Oral Reports • 106
Summary • 113
Appendix • 114
Glossary • 122
Index • 125

About This Book

There's no getting away from it: Every student needs to learn how to write and present written and oral reports. Although it might seem scary, it's actually an important task. Reports are helpful tools for both students and teachers.

For you, the student, preparing reports is a great way to increase your own in-depth knowledge of a subject, making you an "expert" in the field you've chosen to write about. Preparing reports also helps sharpen your powers of observation and your thinking and decision-making skills. In addition, the process of preparing and presenting a report exercises your mind as you brainstorm a topic, research information, put it into a final form for presentation, and present it to your teacher or classmates.

Reports are an important tool for your teachers, too. Reading or listening to your report gives teachers a very clear picture of just what your strengths are as a student. Reports can even let teachers know where you might need some additional help. This is especially important if you're one of those students who knows your subject, but "freezes up" on tests or finds it hard to participate in class discussions. Reports give your teacher more opportunities to see you shine.

This book is a guide to writing and presenting great written and oral reports. In it you'll learn just what teachers look for in a good report. You'll learn different ways to select topics, where to find information, how to take and organize notes, how to transform your notes into a well-written report, and more. You'll find handy charts and checklists to help you through every step of the process, from selecting your topic to handing in your finished draft or making a classroom speech.

Read through this book once without trying to memorize it. Then when you get your next report assignment, refer to this book each step of the way. You don't have to follow each one of the book's suggestions exactly; you can adapt them to your own learning style. Every chapter will give you enough guidance so that you'll soon be on your way to becoming an "Ace Report-er."

Chapter 1 • 5

Me? Write a Report?

You might be surprised to discover that you are already a reporter in some ways. Most of us have had an experience like this: You run indoors to tell your mom that your brother or sister is doing something he or she shouldn't be doing. Chances are, after your mom is able to get you calmed down, the conversation goes something like this:

Mom: "Stop fussing, and tell me exactly what happened."

You: "Well, first I was riding my bike, and then Allie came along and said, 'I want to ride,' and then I said, 'No, it's my bike,' and then she said, 'too bad,' and grabbed the handlebars, and that's when I came in here to find you."

Mom: "Well, we'll just see about that!"

That kind of report had an attention-getting opening, a middle, and an end. The events were arranged in the order in which they happened. And even though Mom wasn't present, after hearing your report of the incident she had a good idea of what took place, thanks to your clear reporting. The report was pretty persuasive, too—it inspired Mom to take immediate action! That's one of the basic ideas behind reports. If you get the readers' attention, inform them, persuade them, entertain them, or convince them of your point of view, you've done a great job!

What's a Report? Why Write Them?

Think of the articles you read in the local newspaper or the stories you watch on the nightly news. The reporters make it possible for you, the reader or viewer, to know all about events that you couldn't possibly have witnessed or experienced yourself. Yet due to the reporters' thorough research and skillful presentation, you are able to learn about occurrences that may have taken place half a block or half a world away, increasing your store of knowledge and enriching your life.

Of course, the reports you prepare for school are a little different from the kinds of reporting described here so far. But there are some similarities. The main similarity is that a good report provides enough information about a topic, and is organized well enough, so that a reader or listener feels he or she has a good understanding of that topic, even though that reader or listener did not do the research or experience the events being reported.

What Makes a Good Report?

A good report is organized; it has an introduction, a body, and a conclusion. A written report is organized into paragraphs. An oral report is also organized into paragraphs so listeners can follow along without confusion, although the listeners might not be able to tell where each new paragraph starts.

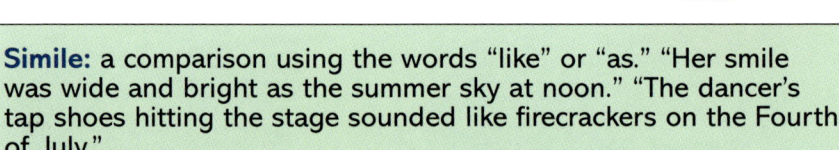

The introductory paragraph, obviously, must tell what the report is about. But it should also grab the reader's attention. You

> **Simile:** a comparison using the words "like" or "as." "Her smile was wide and bright as the summer sky at noon." "The dancer's tap shoes hitting the stage sounded like firecrackers on the Fourth of July."
>
> **Metaphor:** a stronger comparison that does not use the words "like" or "as"; instead, it says that one thing *is* another thing. "His terrified heart was a caged bird, beating its wings against the bars of its cage." "The engineer's arm is a piston, pumping furiously as he loads the coal."

can be sure your introductory paragraph is appealing by using interesting and descriptive vocabulary as well as metaphors and similes.

The body of the report is also written in paragraphs. Each paragraph must be about only one topic, have an introductory or topic sentence, contain supporting details, and contain only sentences that are necessary and related to the topic. (And the sentences it contains must be complete and easy to understand.) In addition, the sentences of each paragraph must be arranged in an order that makes sense.

Just as the sentences within each paragraph must be arranged in an order that makes good sense, the paragraphs themselves must be arranged in an order so the whole report makes sense to a reader. The paragraphs can't jump around from one topic to the next haphazardly; this would confuse the reader. (Remember, the same rules apply for oral reports, which should be written down before they are presented orally. For more about oral reports, see Chapter 12.)

> **Elements of a Good Report**
>
> **Introduction**
> includes a topic sentence that tells what the report is about
>
> **Body**
> several paragraphs that support the topic sentence
>
> **Conclusion**
> summarizes the report and lets the reader or listener know it's at an end

The concluding paragraph of a report must summarize the main points made in the report and also let the reader know that the report is at an end. In addition, every word you use must be spelled correctly throughout your report, and standard punctuation and capitalization are crucial.

If it all sounds a little overwhelming, don't worry. This book reviews many techniques and tools to help you create first-rate reports that contain all the elements discussed here. One of the most important techniques is one you may already know about. It's called "the writing process."

The Writing Process

The writing process is similar for both creative writing and report writing. One or two stages may be slightly different, but the beauty of the writing process is that it's not a rigid pattern. It's a flexible guideline that each writer can adapt to his or her own needs. Whether you are writing essays, stories, or reports, the writing process consists of several general stages.

The first stage is prewriting, which is the process of generating ideas, becoming inspired, conducting interviews, doing research, brainstorming, taking notes—just about everything that happens before you first put your pen to paper (or finger to keyboard) to create the first sentence of the first draft of your report. (Actually, a lot of writing does happen in the prewriting stage, but it's mostly in the

The Writing Process

Prewriting
brainstorming a topic, taking notes, doing research, making an outline

Drafting
putting ideas on paper and turning notes into sentences without focusing on spelling and grammar

Revising
improving what you've written based on your own evaluation and input from others

Proofreading
checking your writing for errors in spelling, punctuation, capitalization, and grammar

Publishing
sharing your writing with an audience, either in final written form (with no errors), in an oral presentation (speech), or in another alternative format

form of taking and organizing notes, not writing your report in its finished form.)

After prewriting comes the outline, rough draft, or drafting stage. This is the stage when you first try out your ideas, writing them down without being too concerned about spelling, punctuation, and grammar. You are just getting your thoughts out and organizing them on paper.

The next step is the revising stage. This is where you try to improve on your first draft. Based on your own evaluation or the opinion of a classmate, friend, parent, or teacher, you may decide to rearrange information, add or take out information, or replace some sentences and words.

Proofreading comes next. This is where you "worry" about all the things you didn't have to worry about in the rough draft stage. Now you check your writing for errors in spelling, punctuation, capitalization, and grammar before going on to make your final copy.

Publishing is the final stage. This is the big time! In this stage, you share your writing with an audience. A written report is only one way to "publish" your writing. Making speeches (or oral reports) and creating presentations with visual aids such as mobiles, posters, and slide shows are some others. (For more information on alternatives to traditional written or oral reports, see Chapter 11.)

The Stages of Report Writing

Writing a report is not very different from writing a short story, essay, or other creative piece. The main difference occurs in the prewriting stage, and it involves research.

When you write a creative piece, you likely generate your ideas out of your own feelings and experiences. In report writing, although the idea for the topic may come from your own feelings and inter-

> **HANDY TIP:**
> This book contains several checklists that can help you complete the various stages of your reports. You might want to photocopy these checklists and keep them near your work station, on your bulletin board, or in a special section of your notebook so you can refer to them easily and quickly when you are writing your next report.

ests, the finished report depends on facts and figures that you must research before organizing and drafting your report. (Doing research is the subject of Chapter 3.)

Research can be fun and easy. Coming up with an idea to write about and turning that idea into a report can be challenging. But don't worry. The next chapter of this book suggests ways for you to generate ideas for report topics; you'll be creating super reports in no time.

Elements of Report Writing

The following activities are involved in creating an effective written or oral report. You might not follow these steps in this order, and you might not follow all of them, but this checklist includes all of the activities covered in this book.

- ❏ Brainstorming ideas
- ❏ Selecting a topic
- ❏ Collecting details
- ❏ Doing research (using sources like books, newspapers, movies, Web sites, or interviews with people who know your topic)
- ❏ Taking notes
- ❏ Writing an outline
- ❏ Writing a rough draft
- ❏ Editing, proofreading, and/or revising your rough draft
- ❏ Publishing your written report or presenting your oral report

Generating Ideas

Now comes the fun part: deciding on your topic. In some cases, your teacher may assign a topic for you. But many teachers feel that students learn more and write better when writing about a subject they've chosen themselves. If this is the case with your assignment, then you're in luck! Look around you for ideas; the possibilities are endless.

Ideas for writing can come from your everyday life and surroundings. The people you live with, the people you meet, the hobbies and sports you pursue—any one of these things can be the basis for your writing. The entire writing process will become so much more interesting, valuable, and fun when you choose a topic that is of real interest to you. It's important, then, to learn how to choose your topics with care.

Where Do Ideas for Topics Come From?

Do you keep a journal? Personal journals can be a great source of ideas for writing topics. Look through your journal and see if any one topic appears more frequently than others. Whatever jumps out at you in this way will probably be something that interests you a great deal, that you've done a lot of thinking about, and that you feel strongly about.

A topic doesn't have to make you happy to interest you; in fact, you may find you have a lot to say about a topic that you have negative feelings about. Great writers have created masterpieces that protest injustice, expose a crime, or attempt to right a wrong. You may be surprised at what you can do with a topic that you dislike, or one that angers you.

Look at books such as Alex Haley's *Roots* and Thomas Keneally's *Schindler's List*. The authors of these works wrote meaningful and interesting books that were essentially reports on difficult, painful, even horrifying topics. (This is not to say you have to write about topics that make most people sad, or that the only good writing is writing about serious, heavy topics. Many upbeat topics can spark worthwhile writing, too.)

Think of a problem you once faced or a difficulty you overcame. Think of the feelings you had about that subject: anger, fear, disappointment, hope, excitement, determination. Did you solve this problem? If so, how? Maybe others would benefit from your experience. Writing about the problem and its solution might make a great report.

Newspapers and magazines can also provide topic ideas. Pick one up and flip through the pages. Look at the pictures, titles of articles, and even the advertisements. You will find lots of topic ideas. For example, an advertisement for a vacation spot might prompt the following ideas:

➤ Family Vacations Can Lead to Family Feuds
➤ People Living in Far-Off Places Have Different Customs Than Americans
➤ The Best Vacations Don't Have to Cost a Lot
➤ The Worst/Best Vacation I Ever Had
➤ The Ten Best Things About Traveling by Air/Boat/Car
➤ My Secret Remedy for Airsickness/Seasickness/Carsickness
➤ Things the Government Should Do to Make Travel Safer

Ideas can also come from your school textbooks. Both words and pictures can inspire ideas. Encyclopedias and other reference books can do the same. When using one of these sources to generate ideas, ask yourself these questions: Why do I want to write about this? What do I already know about this subject? What do I want to learn? How do I feel about this?

Books of quotations can inspire you. Select a quotation with which you strongly agree or disagree. Ask yourself: Do I think it's true or false? Have I had experiences I can write about to back up my feeling? Can I restate the quotation in my own words? Can I illustrate a quotation with an experience of my own? The answers to all of these questions can generate ideas for your writing. (See the Appendix for a list of quotations you can use in your own writing.)

Think about anything currently popular or trendy, such as collectibles, television programs, movies, or celebrities. Special events in your community, or even that old standby, the weather, can be a source of inspiration. But always remember: The entire writing process will be much more interesting, valuable, and fun if you choose a topic that interests you.

Developing Your Topic

Now that you know where your inspiration is coming from, the next step is to brainstorm about it, record it on paper, and start developing it as a topic. You can do this by jotting your thoughts down in a list, writing down anything that comes to mind when you think of your topic. Let your ideas flow, no matter how silly they seem. If you have an idea connected to your topic that you're unsure of, write it as a question. The important thing is to keep the ideas flowing. This is one time when neatness doesn't count!

14 • Generating Ideas

Sample Topic List for a Report on Beavers:

Topic: beavers
Size: about 70 pounds, 2–3 feet long!
Habitat: slow-moving streams near wooded areas
Teeth are orange!
Eat bark. Eat wood?
Build dams
Swim underwater 25 minutes at a time without breathing!
Webbed feet, like a duck
Tail like a paddle
Once hunted for their fur
Who are their enemies?

Or, you may want to try putting your thoughts on paper in another form. One common type of "graphic aid" is a word web.

When you make a list, you jot your main idea at the top of the page and list your thoughts underneath it. With a word web, you write your main idea in the center of the page and write your ideas around it as they occur to you, joining the words to the main idea with lines.

Each one of the topics in the circles of the web can become the subject of the topic sentence of a paragraph in your report. The topic in the middle circle can become your title. (For more information on topic sentences, see Chapter 6.)

One reason it's good to jot your ideas down quickly in graphic form is that it "fixes" them in place so you won't have to risk losing them from your memory when it comes time to write your report. But another reason word webs are useful prewriting tools is that they help you "see" your ideas, allowing you to notice connections you might have missed if you relied only on your memory.

It works like this: As you write each item on your word web or list, that item can help you think of even more items. (When you look at the sample word web and list on these pages, you can probably think of many other items you could add to each.) With a word web, especially, lines drawn between items show how they are related. These lines can help you when it's time to organize your report, because it's easy to see which items should be written about first, second, and so on.

Once you've finished with your list or web, look it over. Put it down for a while, and then read it again. If you think of more details to add, go ahead. A web or list that is rich in details indicates that you have a topic that's worth writing about. (If your list is pretty small, you can always begin again with another topic!)

Sample word web based on a news article in a local paper

16 • Generating Ideas

Charts can also help you think of ideas. Suppose you are thinking of writing a description of something for your report. Write the subject you will be describing at the top of a piece of paper. Underneath, create a chart with five columns, one for each of the five senses. Write appropriate details in each column.

Creating a chart like this gives you plenty of details to write about for your topic: family holiday celebrations. Or, it can help you decide to focus your report on just one of the topics listed.

For example, look at the "Touching" column. Reading about the "Hard, uncomfortable chairs at the kids' table in the kitchen," you might

Family Holiday Celebrations

SEEING	HEARING	TASTING	SMELLING	TOUCHING
• Decorations	• Traditional music, like Christmas carols	• Moist turkey and stuffing	• Savory turkey roasting	• New baby cousin's soft cheek
• Family members in fancy clothing	• Sounds of football game on TV	• Sweet pumpkin pie everyone likes; strange mincemeat pie no one likes	• Onion-y stuffing	• Hard, un-comfortable chairs at the kids' table in the kitchen
• Mom's "good" dishes and silverware	• Uncles arguing about sports; aunts laughing at old stories		• Spicy pies	
• Cousins you haven't seen in ages			• Fruity cider	• Dry turkey overcooked by Grandma
		• Lumpy mashed potatoes with deli-cious brown gravy	• Fresh seasonal flowers	• Grandpa's rough beard when you kiss his cheek
	• Little cousins running around		• Sharp cheese	
			• Hearty gravy	
		• Bitter broccoli	• Aunt Mara's overpower-ing perfume	
	• Sounds of video games from den		• Uncle Ralph's familiar aftershave	

decide to change the topic of your report from a general report on "Family Holiday Celebrations" to "How Kids Feel About Sitting at the Kids' Table at Family Holiday Celebrations."

To develop this topic, you might take a survey of your friends and classmates, asking, "Does your family celebrate holidays such as Christmas and Thanksgiving, or similar holidays from a different culture? If these celebrations include a big meal, do you have to sit at a kids' table? How do you feel about that?" (Don't forget to include in your notes how *you* feel about it.) "Will you have a kids' table at your family get-togethers when you're grown up? Why or why not?" As your questions are answered, jot down the answers in another list, web, or chart. Now you've got a great topic with lots of details for an interesting report.

Now that you've got your topic and you've begun to develop it, you're ready to think about one more prewriting task: determining your audience and purpose for writing.

Why Are You Writing?

All writers write for a purpose. Every time you write—whether it's to provide information, to persuade readers of your point of view, to entertain the reader, or simply to express your own feelings and ideas—ask yourself: What am I trying to accomplish?

It's true that, as a student, your main reason for writing might be "because my teacher told me to." Even if that's your main reason, ask yourself: How can I write to fulfill this assignment?

If your teacher has asked you to write a report on a social studies topic or a book you've read, chances are she's looking for an informational report. If your assignment is to report on your opinion of an issue, you are probably going to be writing a persuasive report. If you are writing a report on an experience, or if you are writing on a theme, then your purpose will be to entertain. (Entertaining writing doesn't have to be funny. Some of the most popular and entertaining professional writers specialize in frightening readers or touching their deepest emotions and making them cry!)

You can have more than one reason for writing. Perhaps you want to entertain and inform your audience. Let's say you are writing a report on your summer vacation in the mountains. You might blend funny experiences (falling into a stream, getting "eaten alive" by insects) with facts about the mountains, such as their height, physical characteristics, animals that inhabit them, and so on. Whatever reason you choose for writing your report, it's important to choose at least one.

Having a reason for your writing helps your personality come through in your words. If there are 26 kids in your class, and each one is writing about the first day of school, there are 26 different ways that that experience can be written about. You see things differently from everyone else, and it's that unique vision that will make your writing unmistakably yours.

Who Is Your Audience?

For a school writing assignment, your audience is probably your teacher and perhaps (especially if your report is to be an oral report) your classmates. (If you were writing a letter, your audience would be the person to whom the letter is addressed; if you were writing a journal entry, your audience would be yourself.)

Whoever your audience is, before you begin to write, ask yourself:
➤ What does my audience already know about this subject?
➤ What might they want to know?
➤ What do I want to tell them?

The answers to these questions will help you decide what information to include and exclude as you write. For example, if you were writing a class report on a candidate running for president of the United States, you would probably realize that your teacher already knows that the United States is a democracy in which people elect a new president every four years. You wouldn't have to mention this fact in your report. However, your audience might want to know information about the current candidates' positions and accomplishments, as well as your opinion on the better candidate for the job.

In a report on elections, you might also want to compare and contrast two candidates. Comparison and contrast is another popular style of report writing. It can be used to write about all sorts of topics, from foods to historic figures to hobbies. Comparing and contrasting, persuading, informing, entertaining: These are among the most common purposes for writing. Knowing what your purpose is will help you write a better report.

It's also very important to know your audience when you're writing a report. Knowing who will be reading or listening to your report will help you select the right language to use in your writing. For example, if you were writing a story for young children, you would use small words and short, simple sentences. You wouldn't confuse them by including too many details. But if you were writing a letter to the editor of the local newspaper, you could use longer sentences and more difficult words. You could include lots of details to support your main ideas, your sentences could be more complex, and your language would probably be more formal.

Now that you have selected your topic, know what details you need to include, know your purpose for writing, and know who your audience is, you're ready to move on to the research stage of the writing process. This is where you begin to add "muscle" to the skinny frame of a topic, creating a "super-strong" report. Let's get busy!

Checklist for Starting the Writing Process

☐ Did I generate a large number of ideas by:
- looking through my personal journal?
- thinking of a problem or difficulty I once faced?
- looking through newspapers or magazines?
- looking through school reading or text books?
- looking through books of quotations?

☐ Did I ask myself the following questions when generating ideas:
- Why do I want to write about this?
- What do I already know about this subject?
- What do I want to learn?
- How do I feel about this?

☐ Did I capture my ideas on paper in one of the following forms:
- a list
- a word web
- a chart

☐ Did I think of many details about my topic?

☐ Do I know my audience?

☐ Do I know my purpose for writing?*

*Of course, one purpose for writing is "Because my teacher told me I had to." But that's not what is meant here by "purpose for writing." Your purpose for writing is what you want your report to do: persuade, give your opinion, compare and contrast two things, and so on.

Research

Research is a funny word. It sounds like it means "search again." What it really means is to look for details that will support the topic you've chosen to write about.

There are lots of different kinds of supporting details—and lots of places to look for them. The ones you select will depend on what kind of report you're writing. In this chapter, we'll look at the kinds of details first and then look at where to find them.

Kinds of Details

Facts A fact is a statement that can be proved to be true. "The Taj Mahal is in India" is a fact. A fact can be checked and proved, either by direct observation and verification (written or photographic), consultation with primary sources (eyewitnesses), or by looking in reference sources, such as encyclopedias, published reports, nonfiction books, or directories.

Opinions "The Taj Mahal is the most beautiful building in the world" is not a fact; it is an opinion. There is no way to prove that the Taj Mahal is more beautiful than all other buildings, because beauty means different things to different people. Whether or not a thing is beautiful is a matter of opinion. When writing your opinions in a report, you must be careful to support them with facts.

Reasons Did you ever ask your parents for permission to do something and then give logical explanations to persuade them that you should be allowed to do it? If so, you already know something about reasons. Reasons are logical arguments for or against a subject. For example, if you want permission to go to see *Space Aliens Among Us!* at the local movie theater, you might try giving the following reasons:

Reasons to See Space Aliens Among Us!

REASON

"It's scientific, about space!"

"The movie director is a creative genius"

"It's half price today"

"All my friends' parents are letting them go!"

POSSIBLE REACTION

Might work, especially if your parents believe in aliens. Sounds like it could be true.

Also might work. Makes you sound intelligent and artistic.

Might work. Parents do like a bargain.

Never use this one. Parents instantly respond with "I'm not 'all your friends' parents!' The only one I'm concerned with is YOU!"

As you can see, some reasons are better than others! The same is true when writing reports. For example, let's say you looked through the local newspaper to get topic ideas. You noticed an article about an animal shelter that was going to be shut down. You decided the topic of your report would be the importance of keeping the shelter open.

In your report, you would give your opinion ("I think the shelter should be kept open because..."), and then use logical arguments and reasons to support your opinion. You would research how important animal shelters are to communities, find out about all the good they do, and how much damage can be done to people and property by abandoned animals in communities where shelters are not available. Those would all be good reasons to support your opinion, and they would make your report strong. (Just writing, "I think the shelter should stay open because I love kittens and puppies," would not be an example of an opinion supported by good reasons.)

Examples These are instances of something that you use in your writing to support a point. Taking the example of the animal shelter, above, you could do research to find examples of communities that used new and different ways to raise money to keep their animal shelters open. Including these examples in your report will strengthen it. In addition, you could also do research to find examples of problems that occur when communities don't have animal shelters.

Sensory Details These add interest to your report by telling how things look, taste, feel, smell, and sound. In the animal shelter report, for example, you might include sensory details that tell how the animals look—their sizes, shapes, colors, and conditions. You'd want to add the sounds of the shelter—the yips, woofs, barks, yelps, meows, and purrs. The clanging sounds of cages and gates, the tones of voice used by the animals' caretakers, and the loving words of people adopting the sheltered pets would also be good sensory details to include.

Stories or Events Your report might include a story retelling an event that supports your opinion. In the case of the animal shelter report, you might consider including the story of a dog that was adopted from a shelter and given to a lonely old man, becoming that old man's best friend and his only connection to the rest of the

24 • Research

community. A story like that would support your opinion that animal shelters do a lot of good for their neighborhoods. Where do all these supporting details come from? Research.

Where Do You Find Sources for Research?

There are many places to find support for your opinions, including:

The Library The librarian will be happy to help you find books, magazines, newspapers, encyclopedias, and other reference sources. It's important to know how to look up information once you find the reference books that contain the facts you need. Knowing how reference books are arranged can help you find facts quickly and easily. Check out the box below for help.

Reference books are specially designed so that it's easy for you to locate the information they contain. Most reference books include:

Copyright page—tells you when the book was printed. This helps you know if the information the book contains is up-to-date or out-of-date.

Table of contents—tells what the chapters are about and on what pages they start.

Appendix—if there is one, it comes after the main portion of the book. It may contain charts, maps, illustrations, diagrams, or extra information about the author or subject.

Glossary—found at the back of the book, it lists special or difficult words contained in the body of the book, defines them, and sometimes tells how to pronounce them.

Index—an alphabetical list of special words and names that are found in a book. It lists all the pages where those words can be found. In a book about beavers, for example, the index would probably contain words such as "dam," "lodge," "teeth," and "fur."

Bibliography—lists books or articles that helped the author in writing the book. (You might also want to look up some of the books listed in the bibliography of any reference book you are reading to get additional details.)

Interviews You can get lots of primary source information by interviewing people who are in a position to know firsthand about your topic. For your animal shelter report, for example, you might interview local politicians or workers at the shelter, or even people who have adopted pets there.

An interview involves more than just asking a few simple questions. You have to be prepared to ask the right questions when you interview a source. Questions that can be answered with a "yes" or "no" are usually not very useful for the report writer. For example:

> Student: "Are you glad you got your dog from the Parkdale Animal Shelter?"
>
> Subject: "Yes."

See? There's not much detail there to add to your report. But if you pose your questions a little differently, you'll probably get more useful answers.

> Student: "How different has your life been since you got your pet from the Parkdale Animal Shelter?"
>
> Subject: "Oh, it is different in so many ways! Before, I had no reason to get out of bed in the morning. Now, I know Muffin needs me to fix his breakfast and take him to the park. Before Muffin came into my life, I felt no

Primary Sources

Primary sources are the people who witnessed or participated in an event, or who recorded their reactions to it immediately after it happened. (Records don't have to be written; they can include photographs, videotapes, computer disks, or audio recordings.)

Primary sources are not necessarily more reliable than secondary sources (reference materials like books, newspapers, magazines, Web pages, and filmed accounts that were written based on the primary source's evidence). You have to check carefully when using primary source material, perhaps speaking to more than one participant or witness to get the complete picture.

one cared about me. . . . I was so lonely. Now, I have someone with me all the time who is happy to see me, who is always there to comfort me, and who guards me and makes me feel safe. Muffin has become my best pal!"

There's plenty of detail there for your report!

Newspapers and magazines are great places to see examples of good interview questions. Make a habit of reading them and taking note of the kinds of questions the reporters ask. See the box below for samples of interview questions you can use as a model for your own interviews.

Asking questions that begin with words and phrases like "When did," "How long," "What's the most/the best/the worst/your favorite," and "What do you want people to know about" can lead to interesting, detail-rich answers. You might want to prepare and take to your interview a sheet of lined paper on which you've written questions using these phrases. Be sure you leave spaces between each question so you can write down the subject's answers. Even if you

Sample interview question starters (fill in the blanks with words that relate to the topic of the interview—the subject's job, an experience, or an event that happened to him or her):

"What's the best thing about <u>(being an animal-shelter vet)</u>?"
"When did you first <u>(realize how important shelters are)</u>?"
"Was there ever a time when you wanted <u>(to quit)</u>?"
"What would you like people to know about <u>(the importance of animal shelters in our communities)</u>?"

plan to capture the subject's answers on audio or video tape, it's good to have your questions written down beforehand. You can always ask more questions as they occur to you during the interview. But having a list beforehand keeps the interview on target, and it can help you get the answers you need for your report.

Searching for Other Sources

You might be surprised to discover all the resources available to help you with your research. Here's a list of some. You may think of others.

almanacs
dictionaries
Internet sites
atlases
magazines
audiotapes

encyclopedias
maps
books
field trips
museums
CD-ROMs

films
directories (e.g., phone books)
television programs
textbooks

The Internet

The Internet is loaded with Web sites that can provide information. The great thing about the Internet is that it's chock-full of informa-

HANDY TIP:
A search engine (like Yahoo!) is a service provided by a company that employs a lot of people who work to sort through Web sites and index them. When you type in the key word you're searching for, the search engine can pull up and show you many of the Web sites they have indexed on that subject. Using a search engine can save you lots of time when doing research on the Web.

28 • Research

HANDY TIP:

If you do happen to get into a site on the Internet that upsets or frightens you, alert your parents or teacher. If someone tries to contact you over the Internet, especially if they suggest meeting in person, do not agree to meet, and immediately let your parents or teacher know. The Internet is full of wonderful information, and lots of good people use it, but not everyone who uses the Internet is friendly or safe. Use common sense and a parent's or teacher's guidance to keep yourself safe when doing research online.

tion that has been placed there by all kinds of people and organizations. Unfortunately, that's also the down side of the Internet. There's so much information it can be hard to find just what you're looking for. Because anyone with a computer can set up a Web site, it's also hard to be sure just how reliable the information is that you find on the Internet.

Here are some Web sites that have proven their value to students and other writers:

Presidential Libraries

http://www.archives.gov/presidential_libraries

National History Day

http://www.nationalhistoryday.org/

The Library of Congress

http://www.loc.gov/

The White House

http://www.whitehouse.gov/

Repositories of Primary Sources
http://www.uidaho.edu/special-collections/Other.Repositories.html

MapQuest
http://www.mapquest.com/

Franklin Institute of Science Museum
http://sln.fi.edu/

Smithsonian Institution Libraries
http://www.sil.si.edu/research

No matter what kind of reference materials you use to prepare your report, the following checklist can help you make sure you get the most out of them.

Research Checklist

- ☐ Did I use more than one source of information: book/Web site/newspaper/magazine? (Try to use more than two books, or, if possible, at least one of each of the above sources, to make sure you get a wide variety of details for your report.)
- ☐ Did I check the copyright dates of the books or videos I used? The dates of the magazines and newspapers? If the books were written more than ten years ago, did I try to find more recent information?
- ☐ Did I write down the title, author, copyright date, and publisher of all the books I used?
- ☐ Did I write down the publication date of any newspapers or magazines I used?
- ☐ Did I take note of the name of any Web site I used?
- ☐ Did I write down the title, director, producer, writer, copyright date, and production house of any films/videos I used?
- ☐ Did I write down the full names of any people I interviewed?

Taking Notes

You've chosen your topic, you've brainstormed details, you know your audience and your purpose for writing, and you've selected and studied your research materials. Now, how do you begin turning that research into writing? You start by taking notes.

Learning how to take thorough research notes will help you create well-written reports that are filled with details. Details make the difference between a skimpy, boring, poorly written report that won't keep your teacher's interest for the time it takes to read it (or your listeners' interest for the time it takes you to present it) and a substantial, interesting report that's actually fun to read (and write)!

Knowing a few things before you begin will help you take useful notes. The main thing to remember about notes is to keep them short. Say you're writing a report on Christopher Columbus, and one of your reference books says: "Christopher Columbus set sail from Spain and discovered the New World in 1492." Your notes should only say something like: "Columbus, Spain to America, 1492."

Although they should be short, they should also include the important facts. Important facts are usually those that tell about the sub-

> Things to remember when taking notes:
> • Keep them short, but include important points.
> • Write them in your own words; don't copy them directly from your resource.

ject and answer the questions who, what, where, when, why, and how. These are called the Five Ws and H, and we'll talk more about them later in this chapter.

How to Take Notes

You can write notes on a pad of paper, separate loose-leaf sheets, or index cards. Some people prefer index cards and loose-leaf sheets because they can physically rearrange them when using them later to create an outline. With practice, you will find the method you like best. Whatever works for you is the method you should use. After all, your notes are a tool for you; no one else is going to see them.

Another thing to remember about notes is that they should be in your own words, not the words of the author of the reference book. Finding your own ways to rephrase what the author is saying is a challenge, but it's the only way to develop your own unique voice as a writer.

One way to get some practice putting ideas into different words is to try playing a game called "In Other Words" with some friends. Whenever one of you makes a statement, the other tries to say it in other words. For example, your friend says, "The 1998 New York Yankees were the greatest baseball team of all time!" You say, "Three years before the beginning of the second millennium, the American League team from the Big Apple proved themselves superior to all others throughout baseball history!" The game continues until one of you is stumped and cannot put the same thought into any other words.

It's a silly game, but it can help you learn an important skill that can serve you well when writing all kinds of reports. Rephrasing another writer's words in your own words (called "paraphrasing") also helps "fix" the thoughts in your mind. It also helps you make sure you really understand those thoughts. Just parroting or copying another writer's words doesn't demonstrate any learning on your part. And as if that weren't enough, copying another writer's words without giving that writer credit is really stealing. You wouldn't want someone else taking credit for your ideas; you don't want to take credit for someone else's. And your teachers don't assign reports to see how well you can copy other people's ideas out of books. Reports are supposed to give your teacher an idea of how you think, and a report can't do that if it's in someone else's words.

Suppose that, in order to prove a point in your report, you absolutely have to include the words of another writer in your report. Well, you can do that if you give that writer credit. Make sure you surround all the words written by someone else in quotation marks. Before you start the quote, announce to the reader that what's coming up was written by another author, and mention the author's name. Tell where you found the quote, and, if the quote is longer than four lines, set it off from the rest of your writing by putting an extra line of space before and after it.

In the immortal words of William Shakespeare in his play, *Hamlet,* "Neither a borrower, Nor a lender, be." Especially when it comes to words! (In case you didn't notice, that's an example of how to use another writer's words in your own writing! Notice the introduction of the author, his work, and the use of quotation marks. It's that easy!)

Organizing Your Notes

In the beginning of this chapter, you read about how to find the important details in a reference source by asking and answering a series of questions known as "The Five Ws and H." They are:

Who?
What?
When?
Where?
Why?
How?

It takes some practice to pick the Five Ws and H out of an article or story. One way to practice is to try picking them out of a familiar story, like a fairy tale or fable. The story of Goldilocks and the Three Bears is one most students know. It's retold on the next page so you can practice picking out the Five Ws and H. Read the story and circle the answers to the questions Who, What, When, Where, Why, and How. Write which question the sentence answers in small

Who? What? Where? Why? When? How?

letters near your circles. Then compare your answers with those on the chart printed after the story.

Goldilocks and the Three Bears: A Crime Story

Once upon a time, in a cottage in the middle of the deep, dark forest, there lived a family of brown bears. There was Mama Bear, Papa Bear, and Baby Bear. One day, when they sat down to eat their midday meal of porridge, the bears noticed that it was too hot to eat right away. "I know," said Papa Bear, "let's go for a walk until it cools." And so they left the three bowls of porridge to cool on the wooden table.

Now it so happened that in this forest there also lived a pretty little girl. She was named Goldilocks because of her beautiful, golden hair. Unfortunately, Goldilocks was as full of mischief as she was pretty. She had been told not to go near the bears' cottage and not to touch things that didn't belong to her, but she didn't always do what she was told.

The day the bears took their walk, Goldilocks was also out walking in the forest. Seeing the bears' cottage, she walked up and looked through the window. "Nobody's

home," she thought to herself. So she just walked up to the door and entered, without even knocking.

Seeing the three bowls of porridge on the table, she ate a little bit from one. "Too hot," she said. She tried another. "Too cold," she said, and tried another. "Just right," she said, and ate it all up.

She tried out the bears' chairs, too. "Too hard," she said, trying one. "Too soft," she said, trying another. "Just right," she said, and whoops! The little chair broke into pieces!

By this time, Goldilocks was tired. She went upstairs and tried out the bears' beds. Again, the first was too hard, the second too soft, but the third was just right! It was so comfortable that she fell asleep, and she was still sleeping when the bears came home. Seeing their porridge eaten and their chair broken, they thought, "We've been robbed! Maybe the burglar is still here and we can catch him!" Carefully, they went upstairs to see if the intruder was still there.

"There she is, in my bed," cried Baby Bear. Goldilocks woke up in alarm, threw off the covers, jumped out of the window, and ran home. She never went back to that cottage again!

> ### A "Five Ws and H" Chart for Goldilocks and the Three Bears:
> **Who:** Goldilocks; Mama, Papa, and Baby Bear
>
> **What:** A crime
>
> **When:** Once upon a time...
>
> **Where:** The bears' cottage in the forest
>
> **Why:** Goldilocks has a tendency to go places and do things without permission.
>
> **How:** She entered the bears' house while they were out. When they returned, they were shocked to find her sleeping there and their property broken and ruined.

You might also notice that many articles printed in your local newspaper are written in this Five Ws and H style. For more practice, try this exercise: Take the first five pages from your local newspaper and select any three stories that interest you. Circle the first paragraph in each story. You should be able, within the first paragraph, to find the answers to the questions Who, What, When, and Where. Sometimes you'll have to read further to find out the Why and How. Notice how the newspaper writers get the important details into the beginning of their articles and then spend the next few paragraphs explaining and supporting those details. In a way, that's what you will be doing with your reports: setting out your main idea and then supporting it with details in a well-organized way.

Creating a Note-Taking Grid

One way to organize the details you've collected after asking the Five Ws and H is to create a note-taking grid. This is an excellent way to organize all your notes so you have them at your fingertips when preparing the outline for your report. Yes, it does mean rewriting all the notes you scribbled on loose-leaf paper or index cards. But the time you spend re-writing your notes on the grid will be well worth it when it comes to writing your actual report, because not only does this method organize your notes, it arranges them in the form in which you'll probably want to use them when writing your final report.

Look at this sample note-taking grid for a report on Dr. Martin Luther King, Jr. By filling in each section of the grid, the writer of this report has a head start on organizing his or her rough draft. All the facts are in order, and the resource materials where the facts were found are right there, ready to be included in the report (maybe even for extra credit!).

Subject of Report: Dr. Martin Luther King, Jr.

Resources	Book, *Meet Dr. King* by Mildred Allgoog, 1986, Apogee Press.	Movie, *The Content of His Character,* made in 1990 by Zenith Films, directed by Alva Barlsow
Who?	Son of preacher, he grew up to be a preacher	One of the greatest leaders of all time
What?	Civil rights leader	Influenced the lawmakers and the average citizens
When?	1960s	1960s
Where?	Mississippi; Alabama; Washington, D.C.	All across the U.S., especially the deep South
Why?	He felt African Americans weren't treated fairly	To bring equal protection of law to all people, so his kids could have a better life
How?	He led marches, made speeches	Used only nonviolent methods

When you prepare your report, refer to the notes you wrote on index cards or paper to help you fill in the grid. In the first box next to the word "Resources," write the complete name of the first resource you'll be using (whether it's a book, movie, interview, or other source), including all publishing information. Then go down to the next box under the "Who" heading. Ask yourself, who did this resource talk about? Look for the answer in your notes.

Continue down that column, writing the answers to the remaining Five Ws and H questions that you discovered in that particular resource. Not every question will have an answer. For example, if you're writing a report on African elephants, you may not have an answer to the Who question. However, you will be able to fill in answers to the What, When, Where, and Why questions. The How questions are not always answered, either. That's okay. Not every topic has a "How." Use the completed grid on the previous page as a model.

Use Two Grids to Create a Compare/Contrast Report

As you might imagine, if you want to create a report that compares and contrasts two topics, you can use this method to prepare two grids—one for each topic.

Persuade with a Grid

If you want to use a grid to prepare a persuasive report, start out with a blank grid and write your opinion on the top of the page. This will be the topic of your report.

This time when you ask yourself the Five Ws and H, you might not find all the answers in your notes. Some of the answers should be supported by research you've written in your notes, but the rest should come from your own thoughts and feelings. Alternate writing information from resources and from your own opinions, as in the sample grid that follows.

Topic: Our Animal Shelter Should Not Be Closed

Resources	*The Daily Citizen,* (newspaper) March 18, 1998	My opinion	My grandpa, interview
Who	Ed Rubenstein, dog catcher	Everybody in our community	John Coombes
What	Has made a study of animal shelters across the nation that showed cases of rabies in dog populations rise 50 percent when shelters are closed	Should be concerned. Rabies is a serious disease that can kill. We should fight to keep the shelters open.	Thinks shelters should be shut down because they're smelly, noisy, and messy
When	All during the 1990s	Especially now, with politicians talking about closing the shelter	Should be shut soon
Where	In cities the same size as ours	Right here in our town	Especially the one near his house
Why	He was concerned about the effects of closing shelters	To protect ourselves and our pets	To let the neighbors get a good night's sleep
How	He looked up his fellow dog catchers in the Directory of American Dog Catchers and asked them to send him reports on the subject	By writing letters, signing petitions, and staging peaceful protests in front of the shelter	Just pass a law against them, lock the doors, fire the workers, let the animals go free, hopefully to other neighborhoods

40 • Taking Notes

Whichever method you use, once you've filled in your grid, look it over. With all your facts laid out in this form, it should be easy for you to decide which are most important and which are not so important, which should definitely be included in your report and which you might want to do without. (Can you pick the opinions in the grid on the previous page that probably should not be included in your report? If you said Grandpa's interview, you're right.)

Now it's up to you to decide which bits of information should go first in your outline and which should follow. Seeing all your research, details, opinions, facts, and reasons collected in this manner should really help you with the next stage of the writing process: creating an outline.

Handy tip:

When using research materials—such as books, magazines, and newspapers—that belong to the school or public library, you must never write in them or circle anything in them. The problem then is, how do you mark the sentences and paragraphs you want to remember to write about for your notes? You can use small self-stick notes. Attach the note to the page near the sentence you want to remember for your notes, and then write on the self-stick note to remind yourself which of the Five Ws or H the sentence answers, or include any other information you might want to remember.

Creating an Outline

An outline is the framework that supports your report. A good outline helps you make sure you don't forget a single thought you want to express in your finished report. Using your note-taking grid as a reference, you can make sure you include all the important details that your research uncovered. Putting them into an outline helps you make sure that nothing you had wanted to include is left out of your finished report.

There are several different ways to organize your outline. For example, if you are reporting on an event in history, you will need to review your note-taking grid to discover what happened first, what happened second, and so on. This is a sequential or chronological report. It's very easy to organize. In fact, this kind of report almost organizes itself.

| Dinosaurs roamed the earth. | Dinosaurs became extinct. | Today, scientists try to find out why. |

But let's say you're writing a report that describes something. Perhaps it's a work of art, an animal, or a sports hero. In that case, you'll need to decide the order in which to write your descriptive report.

You'll need to write the ideas in a sequence that makes sense and enables the reader to understand what you are describing. If you are describing an animal, for example, you might want to start your report with a description of how the animal is born, move on to how it grows, and finish with how it lives as an adult.

42 • Creating an Outline

If you are describing a sports hero, you might talk about his or her most recent achievements and work your way back to the beginning of his or her career. Or, you can start your description at the beginning of your hero's career and move to the present. It's up to you. Whichever you choose, just make sure to stick with that choice. (You might confuse your reader if you move back and forth between time periods when describing your topic.)

When you look over your notes to decide in what order you want to put your details, it helps to think: Can I organize these details from biggest to smallest? Best to worst? Nearest to farthest? Most important to least important? Most recent to most distant?

figure 1

If you used a note-taking grid, you can now go back and, using a different color pen or pencil than the one you used to write your notes, number each detail in the order in which you want to write about it (figure 1).

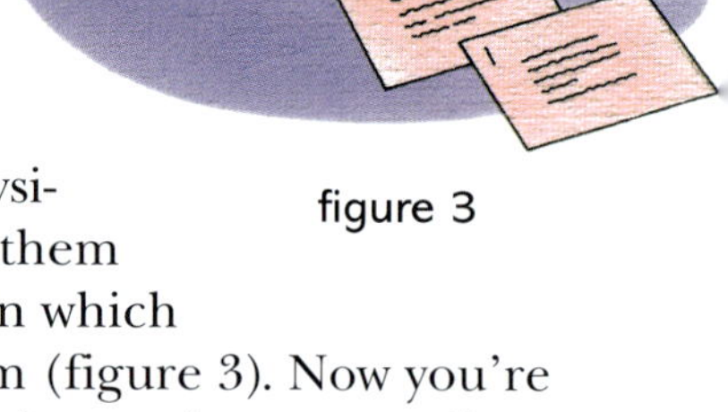

If you didn't use the note-taking grid, but you took notes on paper in a list or a word-web format, go back over them and number them the same way (figure 2). If you took your notes on index cards, go through them and physically arrange them in the order in which you want them (figure 3). Now you're just about ready to write your outline.

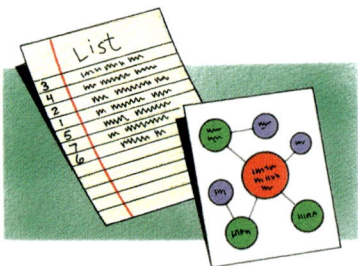

figure 2

figure 3

Several Ways to Organize Your Outline

Depending upon the kind of report you are going to write, there are several different ways to organize your outline. For the chronological or sequential report, decide if you will begin with the event that happened first or last, and arrange your outline accordingly.

Chronological or Sequential Report Outline

Dinosaurs

I. Introduction: What happened to dinosaurs?

II. Dinosaurs roamed the earth

    a. Scientists found fossils, show existence of dinosaurs

    b. Fossils found all over earth, every continent

    c. Scientists can tell age of dinosaur fossils. They know when dinosaurs lived.

III. Dinosaurs became extinct

    a. At a certain point in time, fossils stopped

    b. No dinosaurs today

IV. Scientists try to find out why

    a. Many doing research

    b. Lots of theories, no real answer

V. Conclusion: My opinion based on reported information

This sample outline shows how a chronological or sequential report might be organized. Notice how each main idea follows in time from the distant past (when dinosaurs roamed the earth) to the present (when scientists study them), and ends with the writer giving her opinion at the conclusion.

44 • Creating an Outline

Notice also that the outline is not really written in complete sentences, just sketchy phrases. The sketchy phrases will be turned into complete sentences during the rough draft phase of the writing process. Both the main ideas and details in the outline come from the research that was organized in the note-taking grid, word web, and/or index cards (see figures 1–3 on page 42).

Comparison and Contrast Report Outline

For a report in which you compare and contrast two ideas or items, the outline will look pretty much the same as the sequential or chronological outline on the previous page. You will use Roman numerals for the main
ideas and letters of the alphabet for the supporting details. You'll start with an introduction that states your goal: to show how two items are alike or different.

Examples of comparison and contrast reports might be:

• **Our Modern World Is Much Like Ancient Rome.** This report outline would start out with a topic sentence stating that life in

America today is not so different from life in ancient Rome. Then, Roman-numeral headings would name several areas of life, such as family, work, and school. Each of these headings would be followed by supporting details—

> When writing comparison and contrast reports and outlines, make sure you state all the similarities together and all the differences together. For example, in a report giving your opinion on "Who's the Better Fighter: Muhammad Ali or Mike Tyson?" you might say:
>
> "Mike Tyson and Muhammad Ali are both boxers. They have both been heavyweight champions. They have earned millions of dollars from their skills in the ring, but their similarities end there. Muhammad Ali is the much greater athlete...." Then you'd list and discuss the differences. Don't go back and forth between similarities and differences, or you'll confuse the reader.

lettered a, b, c, and so on—to illustrate the point of the report: that life today is like life in ancient Rome.

- **Muhammad Ali Is a Better Fighter than Mike Tyson.** This report outline would start out with an introduction stating the topic. Then the Roman-numeral headings would probably list several characteristics of what it takes to be a great fighter. The a, b, and c headings underneath would be followed by supporting details to show the writer's opinion that Muhammad Ali possesses these qualities and that Mike Tyson does not.

- **People Speak English in England... Only They Don't Sound Like Us!** The introduction of this report would state the writer's opinion that the English spoken in England doesn't sound like American English. The Roman-numeral headings would point out several differences in vocabulary and pronunciation, and the a, b, and c headings underneath would be followed by examples that the writer has researched by interviewing subjects or reading reference books.

46 • Creating an Outline

Questions to Ask Yourself When Preparing Your Outline

No matter what kind of report you are planning to write—sequential, comparison and contrast, persuasive, descriptive—there are several questions you should ask yourself as you complete your outline.

1. Is my topic sentence clearly stated in my report's introduction? Would someone picking up this report know what I'm going to write about just by looking at my topic sentence in my outline?

2. Is my information arranged in a way that is easy to follow? Does it jump around between time periods, or does it progress smoothly in sequence?

3. If I'm comparing and contrasting two things, did I state all the similarities together and all the differences together?

4. If I stated my opinion, did I support it with facts and details from my notes?

5. Did I end with a conclusion and give the reasons I came to that conclusion?

Alternative Forms of Outlines

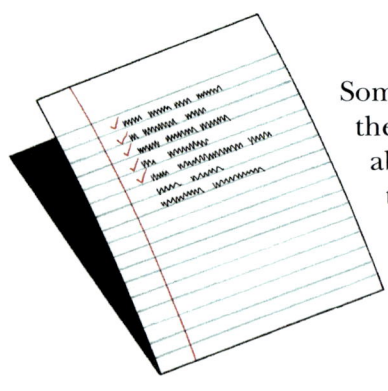

Some students don't feel comfortable using the traditional kinds of outline described above. If it's all right with your teacher, there are some other kinds of outlines that you can use that might be better suited to your individual learning styles. Since some teachers do like to see your outlines as well as your finished reports, it may be a good idea to check with your teacher first to see if it's okay to use one of these alternative outline forms. (Note that although these alternative outline forms will help you organize your thoughts, they are not as useful for developing main ideas and supporting details as the traditional type of outline described above.)

Sequence Outline

You may be familiar with sequence outlines under their less fancy name: time lines. Sequence outlines or time lines are useful when writing reports for a social studies class, because they clearly show events in the order in which they took place.

As you can see, this kind of organization does not clearly show which are the main ideas and which are the supporting details. However, if you feel more comfortable using it, by all means give it a try. Just be sure it's okay with your teacher first, especially if he or she wants you to hand in your outline as well as your finished report for credit.

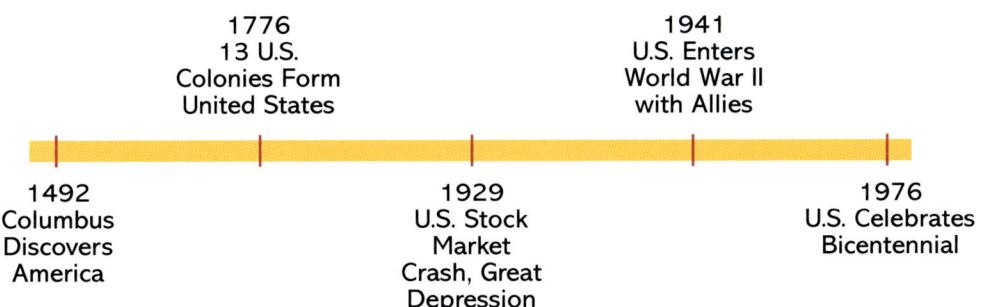

48 • Creating an Outline

Concept Outline

Concept outlines are similar to word webs. You start out by writing your main idea or topic sentence in the middle of a blank piece of paper, and then arrange your supporting details around it. Like the sequence outline, this type of outline does not make it as easy for you to see the relationships between the ideas as the traditional outline does, but many students feel comfortable with it. And if it's all right with your teacher, you may want to try using it.

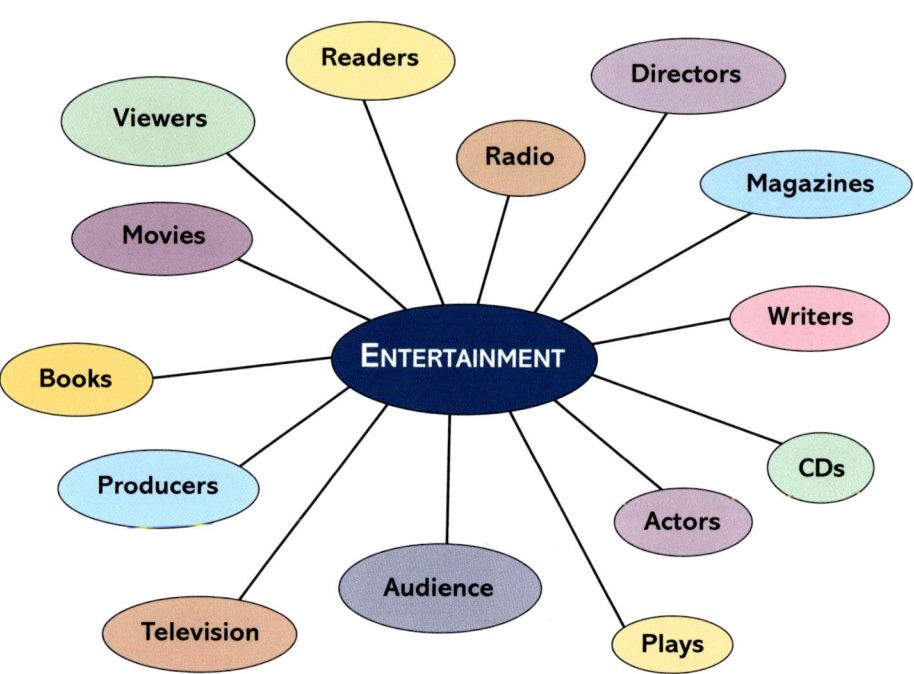

Flow-Chart Outline

This kind of outline is useful for showing the way one idea flows out of another.

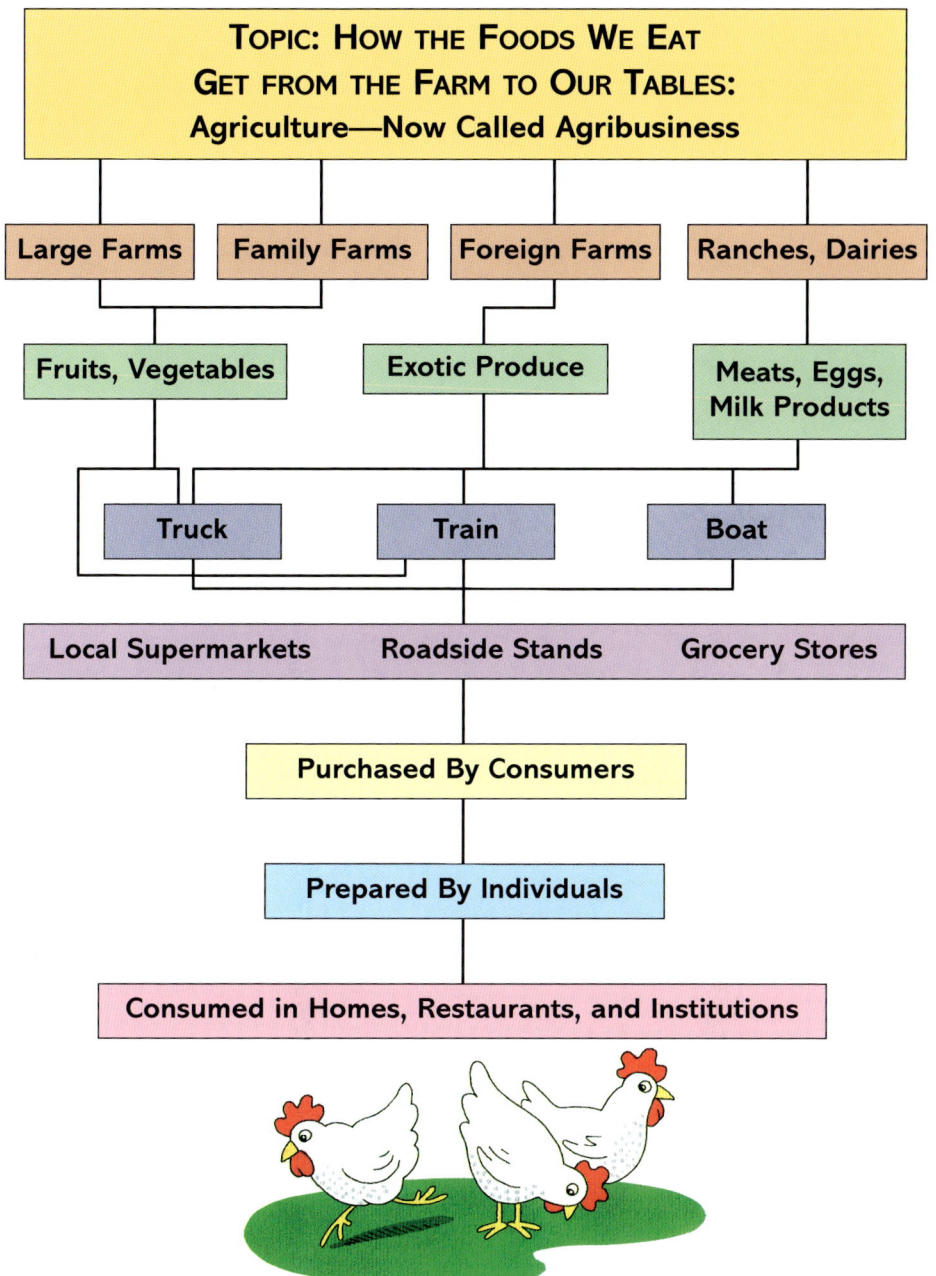

Venn Diagram Outlines

You are probably familiar with Venn diagrams from math classes. You can also use Venn diagrams to create outlines for reports, especially comparison and contrast reports. Once again, check with your teacher to see if this kind of outline is acceptable, especially if your teacher wants you to hand in your outline with your report for credit.

Topic: Skeleton Bones—Compare/Contrast

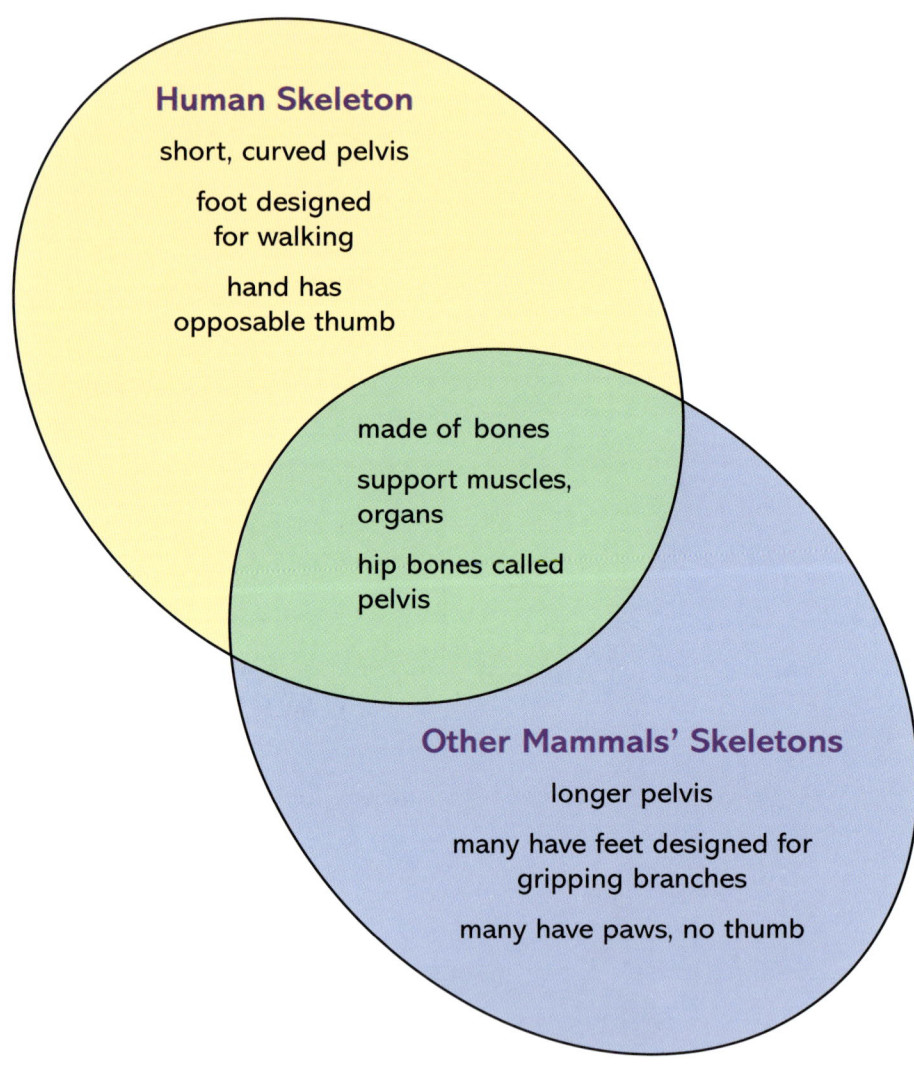

Human Skeleton
- short, curved pelvis
- foot designed for walking
- hand has opposable thumb

(shared)
- made of bones
- support muscles, organs
- hip bones called pelvis

Other Mammals' Skeletons
- longer pelvis
- many have feet designed for gripping branches
- many have paws, no thumb

Creating an Outline • 51

The aspects that are different about each topic are included in their separate circles. The things that are shared between the two topics are in the overlapping portion of their circles.

Whichever way you choose to outline your report, your outline should be a tool that lets you see clearly what your finished report is going to look like. Sometimes, when you finish writing your outline, you'll realize you haven't collected enough detail to make a really thorough report. Then you need to go back and do some more research before completing your outline and moving on to the next stage.

Right about now you're probably wondering why this is called the "prewriting" stage of the writing process! It seems like you've done an awful lot of writing already, doesn't it? Brainstorming ideas, turning those ideas into topics, searching for details, taking notes from research sources, interviewing subjects, and then creating note-taking grids and outlines…when, you must be wondering, do you actually start writing your report? Well, the good news is—soon! And when you do begin to write your rough draft, you'll find that all this prewriting pays off, making it easy for you to complete the best reports ever!

The Introduction and Rough Draft

You've followed the steps in the first five chapters and completed the prewriting portion of your report. You're now ready to begin the true "writing" portion of the writing process. Because of your careful note-taking and outlining, you know exactly what your report will include. Now, all you have to do is write it!

This can be easier said than done. After all, you can't just copy your sketchy notes. That wouldn't make much of a report. You certainly can't go back to your research and copy from your sources. That would be stealing. Whatever you write has to express the topic you've chosen in your own voice, thoughts, and ideas. It's easy to say "just write it in your own words." But what words? This is where knowing your audience comes in handy.

Since your audience is your classroom teacher and possibly your classmates, what you're aiming for when you begin to write your report is a balance between the formal language you probably found in your research materials, and the informal way you speak to your friends and family.

But don't worry too much about finding your voice right at this minute. You're still in the rough draft stage of the writing process, when you don't need to be concerned about writing perfect sentences in just the right voice. In the rough draft stage, the most important thing is to get your thoughts out of your outline, into sentence form, and into your report. Let's start with the basics.

Paragraphs: The Building Blocks of Reports

A report is composed of paragraphs. Each paragraph of a report tells about one topic. Each paragraph has a topic sentence and several other sentences that contain details supporting the topic sentence. And this is when your outline comes in handy. Each Roman numeral of your outline is going to be a paragraph or group of paragraphs in your report; each smaller division within that Roman numeral will be turned into one or a few sentences that support your topic sentence. Now it should be clear why you created your outline: You know exactly what information your paragraphs need to contain, and in what order those paragraphs should appear in your report. Remember, each paragraph only contains sentences that are necessary to support that one topic. (Notice the way all the sentences in this paragraph you're reading have to do with the contents of your paragraphs.)

Each sentence in a paragraph should be clear and make sense. The sentences should be complete and should flow smoothly. It's okay, however, to vary the length of the sentences; some can be long, some can be short. The sentences in a paragraph should be arranged in an order that leads the reader from one thought to another in a sensible manner so the reader doesn't get "lost." The sentences in the following paragraph are arranged in an order that does not make sense.

> **Goldilocks went for a walk in the woods. It was the cottage of the Three Bears. She saw a cottage. She went inside. She saw that the door was open. Goldilocks was curious.**

54 • The Introduction and Rough Draft

Could you put those sentences into an order that makes sense? Give it a try.

_____

_____

_____

_____

_____

_____

_____

> **Answer:**
> Goldilocks went for a walk in the woods. She saw a cottage. It was the cottage of the Three Bears. She saw that the door was open. Goldilocks was curious. She went inside.

The rules for writing paragraphs hold true for every paragraph you will ever write. But when you are writing a report, you will be creating some special kinds of paragraphs that have a few extra rules of their own.

Every good report needs three special kinds of paragraphs: One "introductory" paragraph, several "body" paragraphs, and one "concluding" paragraph. Each paragraph has its own distinct job. And once you understand the duty of each paragraph, it's easy to write paragraphs that perform their functions perfectly.

Let's look at introductory paragraphs first. The word "introduce" literally means "to lead one thing into another." And that pretty much sums up the job of the introductory paragraph. It leads one thing (your reader's attention) into another (your report).

The Job of an Introductory Paragraph

The job of an introductory paragraph is similar to an introduction between two people. For example:

You: "Mom, this is my friend, Ami."

Mom: "Hi, Ami."

Ami: "Hi, Mrs. Nellis."

You: "Ami's a skateboarding expert!"

Mom: "Really? My goodness! Your parents must be worried sick!"

That's the kind of introduction you're probably most familiar with—a way for two people who don't know each other to meet, usually directed by a third person who knows both of them. In a way, that's how an introductory paragraph works in a report. You, the writer, are the third person. You know your audience. You also know your report's subject. In your introductory paragraph, you are going to arrange a meeting between your audience and your subject. It's almost like introducing your friends to your parents.

Now, you probably try to make sure your friends look presentable before you introduce them to your parents, and you probably try to be sure your parents aren't doing or wearing anything too weird when you introduce them to your friends. You probably try to present both of them at their best so they'll make a good impression. You might, as in the example, throw in an interesting detail to add

56 • The Introduction and Rough Draft

> **Criteria for Introductory Paragraphs**
> An introductory paragraph
> - must contain a topic sentence.
> - must tell readers what the report is about.
> - uses interesting and descriptive words.
> - gets the reader's attention and makes him or her want to continue reading.

zest to the introduction and make the two parties want to know more about each other. That's exactly what you are trying to do in the introductory paragraph of your report, too. You want to be sure you present your topic in its best light and make it interesting so your audience will warm up to it and want to know it better.

How to Start Your Introductory Paragraph

There are several ways to start an introductory paragraph so that you get your reader's attention and interest right away. Here are some suggestions:
➤ Pose a problem.
➤ Ask a question.
➤ Use your sense of humor.
➤ Use a noteworthy quotation.
➤ Use dialogue.
➤ Say something out of the ordinary.
➤ Set the scene by describing an interesting situation.

The topic sentences in the following paragraphs are underlined. You will notice that they don't *always* come first in the paragraph.

Inside the cramped submarine, all I could hear was the steady pinging of the sonar and the regular breathing of the pilot and engineer. . . . The pings

speeded up—that meant the wreck was close—and I strained to see beyond the small cone of light that pierced the endless underwater night. . . .

From Ghost Liners, *by Robert D. Ballard and Rick Archbold*

That's an example of setting the scene with an intriguing situation. You can really imagine the tiny quarters of the submarine, and the echoing "ping" getting faster and faster as the writer excitedly peers through the viewport. The spooky, endless darkness of the ocean floor seems to crowd in all around. What will he see? What will happen next? You have to keep reading to find out! That's the way you want your readers to feel.

"Hail, Caesar, those who are about to die salute you."

—The gladiators' greeting to the emperor, A.D. 80–523

The ruins of the Colosseum in Rome still stand—despite many fires, earthquakes and military attacks—as a reminder of the great days of the Roman Empire nearly 2000 years ago. The huge oval amphitheater, which was completed in A.D. 80, could seat up to 50,000 people. It was used for a variety of spectacular entertainments, including gladiator contests, chariot races, and even a mock sea battle, for which the whole arena had to be flooded. . . .

From Amazing Structures, *by Michael Pollard*

That's an example of starting your introductory paragraph with a quote. It's an interesting quote, bringing to mind images of toga-wearing Roman emperors and sweaty gladiators fighting for their lives. The writer uses descriptive words to get us interested in his topic: the Roman Colosseum, which he depicts as being huge, exciting, and filled with action. We want to continue reading to learn more about this colorful place. The topic sentence in the paragraph is the first sentence of the paragraph that follows the quotation, which sets the scene. (See the Appendix for a selection of quotes you might use to start introductory paragraphs.)

> **Sloths are famous for moving slowly.** One mother sloth "hurrying" to her baby took an hour to travel 15 feet! These strange mammals spend much of their lives hanging upside down in trees in South American rain forests. They rarely come down to the ground....
>
> *From* The Ultimate Book of Bones, *by Jinny Johnson*

This is an example of getting the reader's interest by saying something out of the ordinary. An ordinary mother animal would rush to help her baby in a matter of seconds, but the sloth is extremely slow. And an animal that lives in the treetops and rarely comes down to the ground is different, indeed. The writer is hoping readers may be interested in learning more about these truly out-of-the-ordinary creatures. The topic sentence is exactly where you'd expect it to be: at the beginning of the report.

You can use any of these techniques to make your own reports more interesting. When you are doing your research, take note of how the writers of the materials you read try to catch your interest in their writing. Some will no doubt be more interesting than others. Make note of the opening sentences that get your attention, and use those same techniques in your own writing. But remember, use the same techniques, not the same words. You want to express yourself in your own unique voice.

> **HANDY TIP:**
> Even though an introductory paragraph comes at the very beginning of your report, sometimes it's easier to write it after you've finished writing the rest of your report.

A Word About Words

You've been reading a lot about creating interesting sentences and well-organized paragraphs. It's worthwhile to spend a few minutes thinking about the words—especially nouns, verbs, adjectives, and adverbs—that go into creating those sentences and paragraphs. Let's review these common words.

Nouns—words that name things. Proper nouns are the names of specific people, places, and things, and they must be capitalized whenever they are written. Common nouns are words that name general people, places, and things, and they are not capitalized unless they begin a sentence.

COMMON NOUN	PROPER NOUN
building	Taj Mahal
singer	Madonna
championship	World Series
monarch	Queen Elizabeth

When writing reports, use specific nouns whenever possible. Capitalize proper nouns whenever you use them. And if you feel that you're using the same noun too many times, look up the noun in a thesaurus to see if it has a synonym you can use for a little bit of variety. (Some computer word processing programs have a thesaurus built in. Look in your software manual for directions on how to use yours, because each program varies slightly. If you're not using a computer, you can find synonyms in a book like *Roget's Thesaurus*.)

Pronouns—words such as "I, we, you" that can substitute for nouns. If you can substitute one of the pronouns in the first chart on the next page for a word in your sentence and the sentence still makes sense, then use the form of the verb that goes with the pronoun in the table to show "being." For example:

Mammals are warm-blooded animals. They are found all over the world.

Humans are mammals. We are warm-blooded.

Magellan was an explorer. He was a sailor.

Verbs—action words. Actually, verbs do not have to show any really "active" action. Some verbs show "being." Verbs that show being are members of the "to be" family of verbs. They include:

Present tense	Past tense
am (I am)	was (I, he, she, it was)
is (he, she, it is)	
are (you—singular and plural; they; we)	were (you—singular and plural; they; we)

The difference between a verb that shows action and one that shows being is demonstrated in the following chart:

Verb showing "action"	Verb showing "being"
run ("I run five miles a day.")	am ("I am alive.")
sit ("I sit next to Tim.")	is ("He is my friend.")

In the chart above, all four groups of words in parentheses are complete sentences. Each one contains a subject (a performer of action or of being) and a verb (an expression of action or being).

In your report, you might want to use one kind of sentence that seems to break the rule that says each sentence needs a subject and a verb. This kind of sentence usually expresses a command or a request. Some examples of this kind of sentence are:

Close the door.

Turn the page.

Think about it.

The subject in each of these sentences is understood by the reader. Because the writer is telling the reader to do something, it's as if the word "you" is included in the beginning of each sentence. In fact, the subject of a command or request, if not written out in the sentence, is said to be "you, understood."

The following is an example using a "you, understood" sentence in a report (the "you, understood" sentence is underlined):

<u>**Pinch your arm or hand and you will feel the hard bones beneath the skin.**</u> **Lots of different bones make up your skeleton, which is the support and framework for your body. . . .**

From The Ultimate Book of Bones, *by Jinny Johnson*

One reason you might want to use an opening sentence like this is that it immediately gets the reader involved in the subject of your report. It also makes a good "hook" to interest the reader in learning more about your topic.

Naturally, some verbs are more colorful than others and will make your writing more interesting and colorful, too. The same thesaurus that you used to look up synonyms for nouns will also provide you with synonyms for verbs. For example, searching a thesaurus for synonyms for "run" might turn up the following words: hurry, hasten, rush, dash, flee, speed, race, scramble.

You will notice that each one of those verbs has a slightly different meaning than "run." So even though they all mean pretty much the same thing, you could not use any one of them in any sentence as a substitute for the word "run." It's easy to see that "I run five miles a day," doesn't mean the same thing as "I hurry five miles a day," "I dash five miles a day," or "I flee five miles a day." You have to do a little bit of thinking and use common sense to decide when to substitute a synonym for any given word in your writing.

Let's try substituting verbs in a sample paragraph to see how this works. Say you were writing a report on the sinking of the *Titanic*. Such a report might include sentences like the following:

> **The passengers ran through the hallways of the ship. They ran up the steps, trying to get to the lifeboat deck. Most of them were stopped by gates and guards waving guns, but some got through. Those people ran to the lifeboats...**

That's a lot of running around, isn't it? It's not very interesting to read, either. Let's try varying it by using some synonyms that make sense:

> **The passengers hurried through the hallways of the ship. They raced up the steps, trying to get to the lifeboat deck. Most of them were stopped by gates and guards waving guns, but some got through. Those people dashed to the lifeboats...**

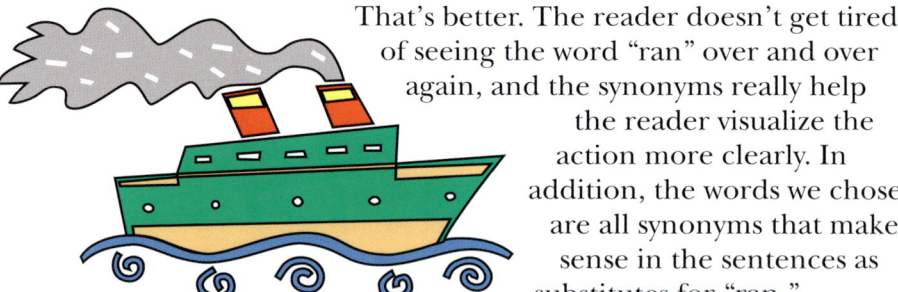

That's better. The reader doesn't get tired of seeing the word "ran" over and over again, and the synonyms really help the reader visualize the action more clearly. In addition, the words we chose are all synonyms that make sense in the sentences as substitutes for "ran."

Adjectives and Adverbs—descriptive words. Adjectives describe nouns, and adverbs describe verbs, adjectives, other adverbs, or other descriptive words. Adjectives often tell how a noun appears to one or more of the senses. Adverbs often answer the question: How or when was an action performed?

Let's try adding some adjectives and adverbs to that paragraph about the *Titanic* and see what results we get. (The adjectives and adverbs in the following paragraph are underlined and labeled.)

The <u>panicky, third-class</u> passengers hurried through the
     adjectives

<u>darkened, narrow</u> hallways of the <u>quickly sinking</u> ship.
  adjectives   adverb, adjective

They raced <u>blindly</u> up the steps, trying <u>desperately</u> to
     adverb   adverb

get to the <u>crowded</u> lifeboat deck. Most of them were
     adjective

stopped by <u>locked</u> gates and guards waving guns, but
     adjective

some got through. Those <u>lucky</u> people dashed to the
     adjective

lifeboats.

Notice the way each new addition to the *Titanic* paragraph—different verbs, adjectives, and adverbs—made the paragraph much more interesting. Try these techniques when writing your own paragraphs to create interesting sentences that really grab the reader's attention. The previous samples demonstrate exactly what a good introductory paragraph should do.

When you are finished writing your introductory paragraph, compare it to the following checklist to make certain it contains all the elements an effective introductory paragraph needs.

Handy tip: When It's Not So Nice to Be Nice

We've been talking about adding zip to your writing by using colorful adjectives and adverbs, specific nouns, and punchy verbs. But there is one word that will make your writing flatter than yesterday's cola: nice.

"Nice" is almost a non-word. It is so overused it has practically no meaning at all. It conveys very little specific information; it doesn't tell how something looks, smells, feels, tastes, or sounds. It just gives a vaguely positive impression. To say a dinner was "nice," or a stuffed animal is "nice," or a birthday party was "nice," is almost worse than saying nothing at all. If at all possible, weed out the word "nice" from your vocabulary. It's just not nice!

Writing Effective Introductory Paragraphs

Does my introductory paragraph:

- ☐ tell readers what my report is about?
- ☐ use interesting and descriptive words?
- ☐ get the reader's attention and make him or her want to continue reading?
- ☐ stick to one topic?
- ☐ have a topic sentence?
- ☐ have supporting sentences that give details and facts about the topic?
- ☐ contain sentences that are organized in a way that makes sense?
- ☐ contain sentences that are complete and written in my own words?

The Body of the Report

You may or may not have written your introductory paragraph when you began writing the body of your report. As the previous chapter pointed out, sometimes it's easier to write the body of the report first and come up with the introduction last. So don't worry too much if you decide to begin writing the body and then go back and do the introduction later. It's your choice.

Just as your body holds you together, supports your head, and helps you do all the things you need to do every day, the body of a report supports the topic of the report. The body of a report consists of paragraphs that tell about the topic that you introduced in your first paragraph. Using your notes, it shouldn't be hard to create paragraphs that do just that.

Let's say you are writing a report on Dr. Martin Luther King, Jr. Your topic (and title) might be "Dr. Martin Luther King, Jr., Was a Great American." In your introductory paragraph, you would create a topic sentence stating your belief that Dr. Martin Luther King, Jr., was a great American. Then, in the body of your report, you'd use your research notes to create sentences that support that idea. (See the note-taking grid in Chapter 4.) The evidence you'd include in your sentences would be based

> **HANDY TIP:**
> Whatever your topic, you should be able to state it in the form of a title for your report, such as "Beavers Are Intelligent" or "UFOs Do Not Exist." Just don't spend too much time in the beginning worrying about a title or a snappy introductory paragraph. It's probably best to dive right into writing the body of your report if you feel more comfortable doing that, and think about the introduction and title later.

on the facts, reasons, and details you organized into your note-taking chart (or whichever other kind of notes you took). You would then be able to build those sentences into paragraphs that you could organize in a clear and easy-to-read report. Refer to the outline you created (see Chapter 5) to make sure you include all the information you had listed in outline form. Keep your information in the same order you did in your outline when you begin writing the paragraphs for your rough draft.

Here's one way some evidence from notes could be built into paragraphs for the body of a report on the topic "Dr. Martin Luther King, Jr. (MLK), Was a Great American":

➤ *Great Americans use their intelligence and skills for the good of others. MLK used his skill as a preacher to make speeches that changed people's ideas about African Americans and their rights.* Then you might list a few speeches, giving examples of MLK's intelligence and skill.

➤ *Great Americans put others' needs before their own. They don't always do what's easiest for themselves. MLK often traveled to make speeches and lead marches when he was sick or tired. He missed his family, but he stuck to his goal.* Then you might give a quote that supports this idea, maybe from an actual person (a primary source) who can tell you what you need to know.

➤ *Great Americans have a vision for this country that makes America a better place to live.* Then you might quote from MLK's own writings or speeches to demonstrate his vision, and talk a little bit about how he changed things for the better by trying to make his vision a reality.

The Body of the Report • 67

Because this is the first draft of your report, it's not really important to make sure you spell every word correctly and use exactly the right punctuation. Right now, you should be most concerned with getting your research out of your notes and onto the page in your own words and in an organized way. (You'll have a chance to "fix" any mistakes in the next stage: revising.)

Of course, if you're just one of those lucky people who is a spelling, grammar, and punctuation whiz, then you may write perfect sentences even in your rough draft stage. There's nothing wrong with that. But some students (and adult writers, too, for that matter) put so much pressure on themselves to create perfect titles and introductory paragraphs that writing becomes a stressful chore for them. It shouldn't be. It actually can be very fun!

In the rough draft stage, you don't have to write neatly, you don't have to dot every "i" and cross every "t." You can spell things incorrectly and even cross things out. The most important thing is to get your words onto the page in an organized form.

> When writing reports for school classes, the first word of the first sentence of each paragraph must be indented. It's customary for the first word to be indented about five spaces from the left margin.

When getting your thoughts out for the body of your report, you do have to be aware of two things: You have to think about what each individual paragraph needs, and what the whole report—which is built out of those individual paragraphs—needs in order to prove your point or fulfill your writing goal.

Each paragraph in the body of your report needs:
➤ to be about only one topic.
➤ to have a topic sentence.
➤ to contain evidence from your research: reasons, facts, quotes, supporting details.
➤ to contain only sentences that are about the topic.
➤ to contain only complete sentences.

68 • The Body of the Report

> to be clear and well organized.
> to be arranged in a good order that doesn't jump around.

The body of the entire report must have paragraphs that are:
> arranged in an organized manner.
> peppered with colorful, descriptive nouns, verbs, adjectives, and adverbs.
> written in your own words, not those of the authors of your research materials.
> filled with enough information so that the reader or listener can understand the topic clearly.
> interesting.

What the Body of Every Report Needs

Each paragraph in the body of my report contains:

- ❏ a topic sentence.
- ❏ complete sentences.
- ❏ only sentences that are about the topic of that paragraph.
- ❏ interesting, descriptive nouns, verbs, adjectives, and adverbs.
- ❏ facts and details that I learned from my research.
- ❏ sentences that are written in my words, not those of the authors of my research materials.
- ❏ all the important information that I included in my outline.
- ❏ a first sentence that is indented.

The Conclusion

You're almost finished with your rough draft! You've created an attention-getting introductory paragraph and well-organized body paragraphs, and you are ready to bring everything to a close. You're ready to create your concluding paragraph.

A concluding paragraph does two things: It lets the reader know that the report is coming to an end, and it helps the reader remember the important points you made in the body of the report by summarizing those points.

To "summarize" means to restate something in a shorter form. Think of it as "making a long story short." You already know how to do this. If you were telling a friend all about a series of events that another friend had told you about, and the school bell was going to ring at any moment, you wouldn't be able to repeat each and every detail your first friend had told you. You would have to give only the most important details. This is what summarizing is all about: retelling a story in a shorter form, but without losing any of the important facts.

For example, your friend Herman was on his way to his baby-sitting job after school when he was hit in the head by a foul ball as he was passing the local Little League field. He was knocked unconscious, and when he awoke, he had lost his memory and now thought he was an opera singer! People passing by heard him singing, badly, on the street corner, and, seeing that he looked dizzy and had a big bump on his head, they called an ambulance. It arrived and took him to a nearby hospital where he was treated and is now resting comfortably after regaining his memory.

70 • The Conclusion

How might you summarize this if telling it to another friend in between classes before the bell rings? Maybe try something like this:

> **"Herman got hit in the head with a baseball and ended up in the hospital! He's okay now, though."**

Think of a concluding paragraph as a way of saying "good-bye" to the reader. If you were talking to your friend on the phone, you wouldn't just hang up on him without letting him know you were almost finished with the conversation. You'd give him verbal clues that would let him know the end of the conversation was coming. You might say, "Uh-oh, my dad wants to use the phone. I'll see you later." Or "I have to go, I have homework." And then you'd say "good-bye" and hang up. (If you made a habit of hanging up without any preparation, you probably wouldn't have a friend for long!)

Treat your readers like friends. Let them know you're going to be "hanging up" or ending the report soon by giving them verbal clues, just like you'd do on the phone. There's nothing wrong with using that old, tried-and-true sentence starter for your concluding paragraph: "In conclusion." Because the word "conclusion" means "ending," your readers will know your report is drawing to an end when they read those words.

The Conclusion • 71

HANDY TIP:
One good way to give the finishing touch to your concluding paragraph is to end it with a rephrasing of your topic sentence.

Here is an example of a strong concluding paragraph from a nonfiction work. See how the author of this piece lets you know her work is coming to a close.

Since 1879, millions of little glass bulbs have come to life. They have spread a light as bright as sunshine and pushed darkness back into the far corners. The miracle is due to Thomas Edison, the great inventor. He worked hard and long to make the lives of his fellow men happier, brighter, and more abundant in many ways.

From Thomas A. Edison: Young Inventor, *by Sue Guthridge*

The use of the word "since" in the first sentence lets you know that the rest of the sentence will summarize things that have taken place over a span of time—the span of time covered by the beginning and middle portions of the book. The next few sentences repeat information about the topic of the book: that Thomas Edison was an inventor whose major invention, the lightbulb, is an important part of life today. The final sentence states the author's opinion (which is supported by the fact that Edison was responsible for many important inventions) that Edison's inventions made life better.

72 • The Conclusion

You can write concluding paragraphs that are strong, too. Let's think back to the example of the report on Dr. Martin Luther King, Jr., from Chapter 7. A concluding paragraph for that report might look like this:

> Notice topic sentence beginning, "In conclusion..."

In conclusion, we can clearly see that the facts about Dr. Martin Luther King, Jr.'s life show us his greatness. Dr. King had great courage when he marched to get bad laws changed. He had great skill as a public speaker when he delivered speeches that we still remember today. He had great vision when he dreamed of a better country for all Americans of every color. And all these things, in my opinion, are what makes Dr. Martin Luther King, Jr., a truly outstanding American.

> Notice sentences that summarize the topics from the paragraphs in the body of the report.

> Notice final sentence is very much like the title and the topic sentence. It brings the report to a close.

Writing Good Concluding Paragraphs

My concluding paragraph contains:

- ☐ information that lets the reader know that the end of the report is approaching.
- ☐ sentences that summarize the main points made in the body of the report.
- ☐ complete sentences.
- ☐ interesting, descriptive nouns, verbs, adjectives, and adverbs.
- ☐ facts and details that I learned from my research.
- ☐ sentences that are written in my words, not those of the authors of my research materials.
- ☐ a first sentence that is indented.

Revision

Whew! Give yourself a pat on the back! You've almost completed the process of writing your report. It seems like a long time since you began brainstorming your topic, then doing your research, taking your notes, and creating your outline. Now that you've completed your rough draft, it's time to bring your report one step closer to completion. It's time to revise.

For some reason, this stage seems to be the one that gives many students a hard time. "Why revise?" they ask. It's as if they feel they've done so much work that when they've written their rough drafts, their reports should be complete. Sometimes students feel so proud of what they've written in their rough drafts that they can't bear to change it. They think, "It's good enough. Why should I change it?" or "My report is full of facts that are correct. It's not wrong. Why should I fix it?"

Well, you *should* be proud of what you've accomplished so far. Maybe it will help if you think about revision in a different light. Don't think of it as fixing something that's broken. Think of it as developing or improving your ideas.

Haven't you ever created something—a drawing, a sculpture, a playhouse, a model, a science project—and then looked at it later and thought of ways you'd do it differently if you had to do it over again? You might have thought of ways you could make it even better. Revision is like that. It's about making a good thing even better.

Sometimes it's easier to revise your report if you put it down for a day or two once you've finished your rough draft. Don't look at it. Don't think about it. Focus on other interests for a while, and then come

74 • Revision

back and reread it with fresh eyes. Read it slowly. Read it out loud to yourself or to a parent, another relative, or a friend. Ask friends or parents to read it to themselves, and then ask for their reaction. Ask them if they understand what you've written or if there's anything that confuses them. Discuss with them what you could include to make your report easier to understand. This is not cheating! Now is the perfect time to use your own opinion and to get the opinion of others you respect, whether they are adults or other students, to improve your finished product. Use this time to your best advantage!

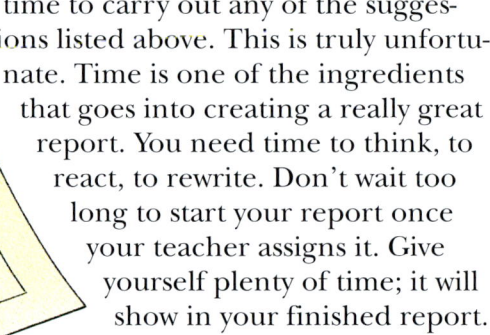

Unfortunately, many students wait until the last minute before their report is due to even begin the process of writing it. Then the due date arrives and they haven't got the luxury of time to carry out any of the suggestions listed above. This is truly unfortunate. Time is one of the ingredients that goes into creating a really great report. You need time to think, to react, to rewrite. Don't wait too long to start your report once your teacher assigns it. Give yourself plenty of time; it will show in your finished report.

How to Revise

Revision is more than just copying your rough draft over neatly. The word "revise" literally means "see again," and when you revise your rough draft, you start by "seeing" it over again. When you look at it this time, you want to see certain things. You need a good introductory paragraph, one that gets your attention and makes you want to continue reading. You want to see that the body of the report makes sense. You want to see sentences and paragraphs that are organized in a way that's easy to understand. You want to see a good concluding paragraph. You want to see dramatic, colorful words that give your writing excitement and life. You want to see words that are spelled and capitalized correctly, and sentences that are complete and grammatical. If you don't see these things, now is the time to include them.

You don't want to see information that seems out of place or that has nothing to do with the topic. You don't want to see paragraphs that jump around, making your ideas hard to follow. You don't want to see the words of some other author copied right out of a research book. And there should not be any misspellings, bad or missing punctuation, or incomplete or ungrammatical sentences. If you do see these things, now is the time to correct them.

But revision isn't just about fixing things that are wrong. Revision is a chance to make your writing express what you want it to express more clearly. Even if you are one of those gifted writers whose first drafts are naturally clear, well organized, and perfectly spelled, capitalized, and punctuated, your report can still benefit from revision. You can use the revision checklists in this chapter to make sure the ideas you expressed in your rough draft say exactly what you want them to say. You can change the vocabulary you used to express yourself more clearly. There is always a better way to write something, and revision is the process of finding that better way.

Tips for Revising

➤ Use dialogue, describe a dramatic situation, or start with a quote about your topic to begin your introductory paragraph and get your reader's attention.

➤ Add details. Don't just write, "I have a dog." Write, "I have a tiny, tan-and-cocoa, blue-eyed mutt named Dingo who looks like a delicious little chocolate-chip cookie with four legs and a tail."

➤ Change some verbs to action verbs. Don't just write, "Houdini came back from Europe to be with his mother." Write, "Houdini raced frantically back from Europe to visit his beloved mother one more time before she died."

➤ Describe what the characters in the report are feeling. Tell what the weather was like if you are writing a report about an event or people that are outside.

➤ Use similes, metaphors, adjectives, adverbs, action verbs, and specific nouns.

➤ And most important: Give yourself enough time to do a thorough job. Start working on your report soon after your teacher assigns it to you. Don't delay.

Revision Checklist

Ask yourself these questions when you are revising your rough draft:

- ☐ When I read my report over, did it make sense to me?
- ☐ When I asked my buddies or parents to read it, did it make sense to them?
- ☐ If it did not make sense to them, what questions did they have?

_____

_____

- ☐ Did I fix my report so that it answered those questions?
- ☐ Did I use interesting words?
- ☐ Did I create an interesting introductory paragraph?
- ☐ Did I use metaphors and similes to create interest?
- ☐ Does my report show that I know the difference between facts and opinions?
- ☐ If I gave my opinion, did I back it up with facts from my research?
- ☐ Did each paragraph have a topic sentence and several supporting sentences?
- ☐ Is my report about one main idea?
- ☐ Did it include verbal clues that the end was coming, a summary of the main idea, and a final sentence that tied the whole report together?

Editing and Proofreading

You have completed the general revision process by this time. You've made sure your report is well organized, detailed, and contains all the important elements it needs to be a truly complete report. Now it's time to perform two more important parts of the revision process: editing and proofreading.

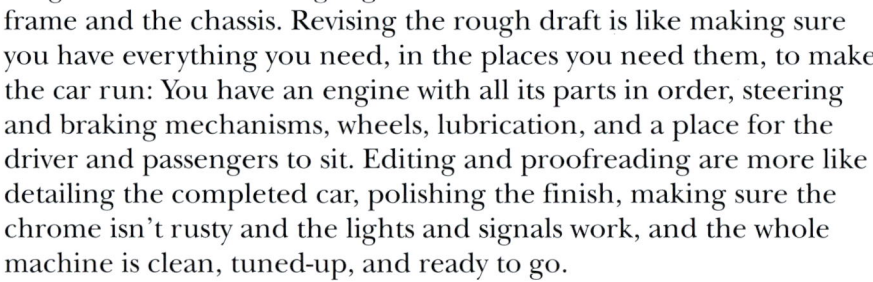

Editing and proofreading are much more specific than the general revising you learned about in the last chapter. Think of it like this: Writing your report is like building a car. Writing the rough draft is like bolting together the frame and the chassis. Revising the rough draft is like making sure you have everything you need, in the places you need them, to make the car run: You have an engine with all its parts in order, steering and braking mechanisms, wheels, lubrication, and a place for the driver and passengers to sit. Editing and proofreading are more like detailing the completed car, polishing the finish, making sure the chrome isn't rusty and the lights and signals work, and the whole machine is clean, tuned-up, and ready to go.

What Do You Look for When Editing and Proofreading?

It can be difficult to edit your own work. Here are some techniques that can help.

Spelling If you are unsure of the spelling of any word, circle it and look it up in a dictionary.

Punctuation Look at every sentence. Does it begin with a capital letter and end with the proper punctuation—either a period, an exclamation mark, or a question mark?

Look at Your Sentences Are any of them too long? If so, break them up into two sentences, making sure each one is complete and has a subject and a verb. If any are incomplete or too short, fix them by inserting a verb, if necessary, and proper punctuation.

In order to make sure your sentences are written correctly, in standard English and with correct spelling, punctuation, and grammar, it's a good idea to review a few grammar concepts. You have probably already learned about these concepts in class, but let's take another look to help you revise your report.

Some Common Spelling Monsters

Correct spelling is important. If everyone just spelled words the way they felt like spelling them, pretty soon no one would be able to understand what anyone else was writing. It's very important to spell words correctly so your readers understand you.

This is another area of writing where reading will help you. Reading professionally written books, newspapers, magazines, and textbooks will expose you to correct, standard English spelling. The more familiar you become with correct spelling, the easier it will be for you to use it in your own writing. If you want to become a good writer, one of the best things you can do for yourself is become an enthusiastic reader!

It would be impossible to try to present, in one small chapter, the rules for spelling each and every word that you're likely to use in your reports. Every writer seems to have certain "problem" words—

there are just too many to cover. However, there are a few words in the English language that seem to cause problems for just about everybody—even the most experienced writers. We'll talk about those words here.

One of the most commonly misspelled words in the English language is a very tiny word with only three letters. Actually, these same three letters can spell either of two words: its and it's.

"Its" and "it's" are examples of what are called "homophones." ("Homo-" means "same" or "alike," and "-phone" means "sound.") Although these words sound alike when spoken, they look different when written down and they have different meanings, too: "Its" (no apostrophe) is the possessive form of the pronoun "it"; "it's" (with an apostrophe) is a contraction meaning "it is."

If you are in doubt as to which one of these homophones is correct, ask yourself about the meaning of the word in the context of the sentence. For example:

1. The baby bird fell out of its nest.

2. I put it back in, and it's all right now.

In sentence one, the nest belongs to the baby bird. The word "its" in this sentence is possessive, therefore it does not use an apostrophe.

In sentence two, "it's" means "it is." The sentence would make sense if we substituted the words "the baby bird is" for the word "it's." We need to use the word with an apostrophe.

So many people have problems with this little word because most words that show possession use an apostrophe. Think about it. If you were to write about something (say, a video game) that belonged to a person (say, a girl named Niki), you would write: Niki's video game. You would use an apostrophe to show possession.

The same is true for many other possessive nouns: Jon's boat; Mr. Wilson's fence; the neighbor's yard. It's (it is) no wonder that people mix up the two words "it's" and "its." The best way to prevent having problems with this homophone is to memorize the two forms, their correct spellings, and their uses so you can use them correctly in your own writing.

"It's" is an example of a contraction. To "contract" means to "shorten" or "pull together." We use many contractions in the English language, and they often cause spelling problems. They include:

Contraction	Original Words
aren't	are not
don't	do not
can't	cannot
haven't	have not
couldn't	could not
I've	I have
he'd, he's	he had (or he would), he is
she'd, she's	she had (or she would), she is
what's	what is
who's	who is

Contractions use apostrophes. Apostrophes are punctuation marks that show where a letter or letters have been removed or left out. The two original words are "pushed together" to make one.

Punctuation

An apostrophe is one type of punctuation mark. The other most commonly used punctuation marks are commas, periods, question marks, and exclamation marks. Each complete sentence you write must end with a period, question mark, or exclamation mark. There are other forms of punctuation, but for your report-writing purposes those will probably be sufficient—at least until you become a really experienced report writer.

A period comes at the end of a sentence that makes a statement. (Just like this sentence.) A question mark is used at the end of a sentence that asks a question. (But you already knew that, didn't you?) And an exclamation mark (!) is used to show excitement. Use exclamation marks sparingly. Let's face it, we all want our reports to be interesting, but very little of the information contained in a well-written school report is so exciting it would be worthy of an exclamation mark.

> **Just because a group of words. Starts with a capital letter. And ends with a period, that doesn't mean it's a sentence. It could be something called a "sentence fragment," just like the three groups of words at the beginning of this paragraph.**

Sentence fragments must often be combined or reworded in order to form proper sentences. Try to fix the sentence fragments from the paragraph above on the lines provided on the next page.

Editing and Proofreading • 83

> **Answer:**
> Just because a group of words starts with a capital letter and ends with a period, that doesn't mean it's a sentence.

First, Let's Agree: Subject-Verb Agreement

We've spoken about making sure sentences are complete and correctly capitalized and punctuated. That's important. But there's another important item to look for when editing the sentences in your report: subject-verb agreement. This means that subjects and verbs in sentences have to agree in number. If one is plural, then the other must be plural; if one is singular, the other must be, too.

You remember that verbs are words that show action or being, and that each sentence must have one. Each sentence must also have a subject: a person, place, or thing that does the action expressed by the verb.

In the short sentence, "Horses run," the subject is "Horses" and the verb is "run." You can see that the subject is plural and the verb is, too. In the sentence, "A boy runs," the subject (boy) is singular, and the verb (runs) is singular. Most short sentences are easy to figure out.

> **HANDY TIP:**
> Make sure your report contains complete sentences by checking to see that every sentence contains a subject (a person, place, or thing) that performs the action or "being" expressed by the verb (action word or form of the verb "to be").

However, there are times when the subject of a sentence is separated from the verb by a phrase. In that case, it's sometimes difficult to tell which word is the subject. Because the real subject is far away from the verb, sometimes we think a word in the phrase that is closer to the verb is the subject, when it is not. This can cause a problem if the word in the phrase, which we think at first is the subject, is different in number from the real subject. We might use the wrong form of the verb. For example:

A <u>description</u> of the burglars <u>hangs</u> on the wall of the post office.

This sentence has a phrase between the subject and the verb. The subject and verb are underlined here. The subject of this sentence is not "burglars," it's "description," even though "burglars" is a noun and it is closer to the verb in the sentence. "Description" is singular and "burglars" is plural. Therefore, even though the word "burglars" is closer to the verb, we must make sure to use a verb that is singular—"hangs."

To figure out what the subject of a sentence is, first find the verb and then ask yourself, "Who or what is doing this action?" In the sentence above, if you find the verb—hangs—and then ask yourself "who or what hangs?" it will lead you to see that "a description" hangs, not "the burglars." This differentiation is extremely important because one noun is singular, the other plural.

Try finding the subject in these sample sentences:

1. The theme of the party is "A Walk in the Clouds."

2. The cost of the gifts is more than one thousand dollars.

3. Every one of the boys has a role to play.

4. The design on the notecards is beautiful.

> **Answers:**
>
> 1. theme, 2. cost, 3. one, 4. design. Note that all of the subjects are singular.

Make sure you don't get fooled by sentences that have phrases between the subject and the verb.

Another kind of sentence that can be a little tricky is a sentence that starts with the words "here," "there," or "where." These sentences sometimes give writers trouble because the verb usually comes first and is followed by the subject. But the same rules apply: If the verb is plural, the subject must be plural. If the verb is singular, the subject must be singular. For example:

> **Here are the tickets.** (The subject is "tickets," which is plural. Therefore, the verb must be plural—are.)
>
> **There is the necklace.** (The subject is "necklace," which is singular. Therefore, the verb must be singular—is.)
>
> **Where is my soda?** (The subject is "soda," which is singular. Therefore the verb must be singular—is.)

There are many more kinds of sentences, words, and phrases that might give you a little trouble when you are trying to make subjects and verbs agree. If you haven't learned about them in class yet, you probably will sometime soon. This book can only mention a few of them and give you some ideas for writing them correctly.

There is one other kind of word that can cause problems when you are trying to make sure your sentences have subjects and verbs that agree. These words are called "indefinite pronouns."

Indefinite Pronouns

You know that a pronoun takes the place of a noun. And you can probably figure out that an indefinite pronoun would be a pronoun that isn't definite, exact, or specific.

Indefinite pronouns are words such as anyone, everyone, no one, some, one, someone, and none. It figures that if a pronoun isn't about a specific person, place, or thing, it might be hard to tell if the pronoun needs to be paired with a singular or a plural verb. The best thing you can do is just remember which indefinite pronouns take singular verbs and which take plural verbs.

Here's a list of indefinite pronouns that tells you which ones are singular and which ones are plural. Use it when you edit your report.

PLURAL INDEFINITE PRONOUNS	SINGULAR INDEFINITE PRONOUNS	INDEFINITE PRONOUNS THAT CAN BE SINGULAR OR PLURAL
several	everybody	all
few	somebody	any
many	everyone	none
both	anyone	some
others	each	most
	either	
	neither	
	one	
	someone	
	anybody	
	no one	
	nobody	

Editing and Proofreading • 87

A Capital Idea

You already know that every sentence must begin with a capital letter. But some other words in sentences should also be capitalized: proper nouns and proper adjectives.

Proper Nouns

What's a proper noun? Well, you know that a noun is the name of a person, place, or thing. Dog, chair, building, road, actor, and desert are all nouns. Another name for them is "common nouns," since they do not name specific people, places, or things.

The following is a list of proper nouns that compare to the common nouns above: Benji, Brancusi chair, Empire State Building, Route 66, Leonardo DiCaprio, Mojave Desert.

Other proper nouns include: days of the week; months of the year; names of holidays, like New Year's Day or Independence Day; names of planets, such as Mercury; and names of cities, states, and countries.

When proper nouns appear in a sentence, they must be capitalized, just like the first word of the sentence. "Michael Jordan played basketball in Chicago, Illinois."

Proper Adjectives

In addition to proper nouns, proper adjectives need to be capitalized when they appear in a sentence. Proper adjectives describe people, places, or things. Common adjectives also describe, but in a different way. In the following sentence, there is one common adjective and one proper adjective. Each one is labeled. See if you can figure out what's different about them.

Axel is a <u>wonderful French</u> chef.
common adjective, proper adjective

The word "wonderful" is not capitalized, but "French" is. French refers to the people of a certain nationality. Names of nations are proper nouns, and words that describe languages and nationalities are proper adjectives. Names of languages or nationalities, such as Spanish, are also proper adjectives. So are brand names, such as Nike and Pepsi.

Titles—A Game of Their Own

Capitalizing words in titles is sometimes tricky. When you write the title of your report, capitalize the first word and every important word of the title. How do you know which words are important? Verbs are important. If there are verbs in your title, they most likely convey important information about the subject of your report, and they must be capitalized. This is true even if the verb is as short as "is." Remember that "is" is a form of the verb "to be."

Of course, there are really no unimportant words, but some words are less important than others. These less-important words are called prepositions and articles. Some examples are listed in the box to the right. When they appear in the title, unless they are the first word of a title, do not capitalize them. In the title, "A Walk in the Clouds," capitalize "A" because "A" is the

PREPOSITIONS	ARTICLES
to, from,	a
between, before,	the
of, for,	an
above, below,	
at, on, upon,	
beyond, beneath,	
under, over,	
around, through	

first word. In "A Dollar a Day," the second "a" is not capitalized, but the first one is. You'll often find that books and magazines decide on different ways to capitalize prepositions in titles. The publishers of this book have decided that all of their titles will have capitalized prepositions when they contain four or more letters, while shorter prepositions are not capitalized. For your purposes, it's easier just to remember to make all prepositions lowercase.

You Can Quote Me

There's another kind of sentence that you might use in your report: a quote. A quote is composed of the direct words of another speaker or writer that you use in the body of your report. Quotes are like salt—a little bit gives your writing flavor, but used too liberally, quotes spoil your writing, just as too much salt will spoil the flavor of good food.

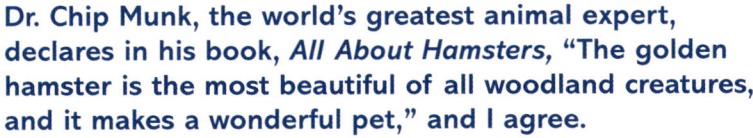

If you do decide to use quotes, remember to set them off from the other sentences by using quotation marks. Quotation marks are like two pairs of floating commas that surround the quotation you choose. Always tell who said the words you are quoting, and, if possible, tell where you found them:

> Dr. Chip Munk, the world's greatest animal expert, declares in his book, *All About Hamsters,* "The golden hamster is the most beautiful of all woodland creatures, and it makes a wonderful pet," and I agree.

Notice that a comma goes after the last word of the sentence right before the quote begins. There are quotation marks before and after the words of Dr. Chip Munk, and the first word of his quote is capitalized, because it was the beginning of his sentence, even though it appears inside a sentence written by someone else.

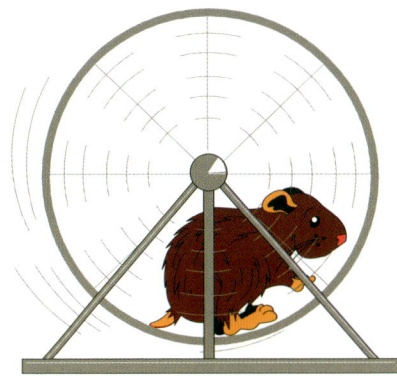

However, after Dr. Chip Munk's words, there's a comma, not a period. The quote is followed by another set of quotation marks, and the conclusion of the writer's sentence. The period comes at the end of the writer's sentence containing the quote, not at the end of the quote itself (unless you were finishing your own sentence with the other writer's quote).

Another way to use a quote is to start the sentence with the quote instead of your words. For example:

"No matter what some so-called animal experts would have you think, golden hamsters are vicious, destructive rodents," said Dr. Ida No. She is one of the leading opponents of Dr. Chip Munk's campaign to save the golden hamster.

Notice that the sentence above started with a quotation mark, then the first word of the quote began with a capital letter. There is a comma at the end of Dr. No's quote, a final set of quotation marks, and finally the writer's words, which are followed by a period. The

HANDY TIP:

You will find it easier to proofread your report if you leave spaces between each line of writing. If you write your report in longhand on paper, just skip a line between each line you write. If you write your rough draft using a computer or typewriter, set the line spacing to at least one and a half. Most teachers prefer that you use double-spaced typing. This will give you space to make your corrections. And, when your report is complete and handed in, the double spacing will give your teacher room to write comments about what you've written.

speaker of the quote, Dr. No, was identified. That's the correct way to include quotations in your reports.

Using quotations can spice up your writing. Don't be afraid to use them because you think you won't remember how to punctuate and capitalize them correctly. You can refer to this book as your guide when including quotations in your report.

Another interesting and easy way to see good examples of well-written quotes every day is to read your local newspaper. Make a habit of reading the paper and imitating the way you see quotations handled in the articles you find there.

In fact, reading newspapers and nonfiction books even when you're not assigned to do a report on them is a great way to learn how to write like professional writers. Notice how news reporters, essayists, and authors organize, punctuate, and capitalize their stories, and look at the kinds of sentences they use. All of this can help you when it comes to writing and revising your own reports.

Did You Notice?

In the example showing how to write direct quotations correctly, the name of the book was included in the sample sentence. *All About Hamsters* was the title mentioned, and it was written in italics. When you name books, songs, poems, movies, or other works of art in your writing, you need to set the title of the artwork apart from the rest of your writing. There are several ways to do this.

Use italics to set off titles of books, names of newspapers or magazines, movie titles, long poems, and names of television shows.

Use quotation marks to set off the titles of chapters from books, articles from magazines and newspapers, or episodes of television shows.

For example:

I love the "Rye Bread" episode of *Seinfeld*.

Gone With the Wind is my mother's favorite movie.

I finished reading up to "The Clue in the Staircase" in *Great Mysteries of English*.

You should read *Manor Houses* by Lady Siddoverthere.

I learned that Leonardo DiCaprio is a natural blonde by reading "The Truth About Leo," in *Teens Monthly*. However, my best friend read an article in *Sassyteen* that was called "Leo Dyes His Hair!"

If you write your reports on a computer, follow the instructions in your word-processing program's manual to change regular type to italic type. If you type your report on a typewriter or write it by hand, however, there's no easy way to create italics. The accepted rule in those cases is to draw a solid line under the words that are supposed to be in italics.

Editing and Proofreading • 93

Editing Marks

We've been talking a lot about what to look for when you revise your report. But how do you indicate to yourself the changes that you want to make? Or, if you're being a revision "buddy" to someone else, how do you show the writer where to make changes? You can cross out words that don't belong and write in new and better words in the margin or along the edges of a page. But sometimes your rough draft gets hard to read with a lot of corrections scribbled on it.

There are some shorthand symbols that can help you revise your report without having to write too many words on top of what you've already written. These are called "proofreader's marks." There are many, many professional proofreader's marks, but even if you only learn a few of them, they can be useful tools for writing and revising your own or a buddy's work.

Sometimes proofreader's marks are used in combination, depending on what has to be done to make the error correct. See the sample on the next page for an example of how to use proofreader's marks in revising your own or anyone else's work.

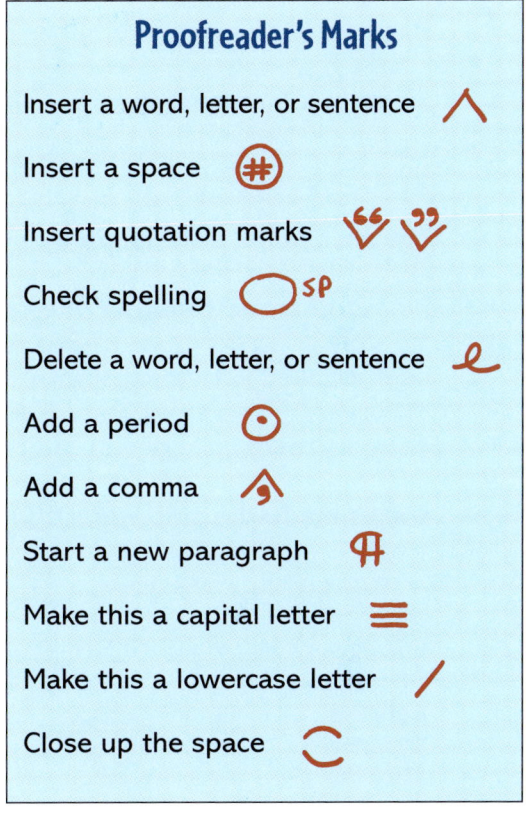

Proofreader's Marks

Insert a word, letter, or sentence ∧

Insert a space #

Insert quotation marks ❝ ❞

Check spelling sp

Delete a word, letter, or sentence ℓ

Add a period ⊙

Add a comma ˏ

Start a new paragraph ¶

Make this a capital letter ≡

Make this a lowercase letter /

Close up the space ⌒

94 • Editing and Proofreading

Egyptians the world's First Sea Lords

We think of the Desert wen we think of Egypt. But the egyptions were also good sailers They learned to sail on ther iver Nile which flowed through their desert land. They built ships out of wood and papayas. Papyrus grew along the banks of the nile, but the wood was imported from Lebanon. Lebanon is a country near Egypt with has lots of cedar trees. The hulls of the egyptian ships were made by using pegs to attache planks of wood together, the cracks between the planks were cawked with a substance made of mashed-up papyrus reeds mixed with oil. Stuffing this into the cracks made the ship watertight.

The way the ships were built was very smart.

This is what your corrected paragraph would look like once you finished revising it:

Egyptians: the World's First Sea Lords

We think of the desert when we think of Egypt, but the Egyptians were also good sailors. They learned to sail on the river Nile, which flowed through their desert land. They built ships out of wood and papyrus. Papyrus grew along the banks of the Nile, but the wood was imported from Lebanon.

The way the ships were built was very smart. The hulls of the Egyptian ships were made by using pegs to attach planks of wood together. The cracks between the planks were caulked with a substance made of mashed-up papyrus reeds mixed with oil. Stuffing this into the cracks made the ship watertight.

Editing and Proofreading a Report

Ask yourself these questions when you are editing your rough draft:

- ❏ Is each sentence complete and grammatically correct?
- ❏ Do the subjects and verbs in my sentences agree in number?
- ❏ Are all proper nouns and adjectives capitalized?
- ❏ Is the first word of each sentence capitalized?
- ❏ Does each sentence end with the proper punctuation mark (period, question mark, or exclamation mark)?
- ❏ If I quoted a source, did I include the quote inside quotation marks?
- ❏ Did I give credit to the author or speaker of each quote I used?
- ❏ If my report is handwritten, is my writing neat and easy to read?
- ❏ Did I use apostrophes in contractions correctly?
- ❏ Can I substitute more colorful words (adjectives, adverbs, nouns, and verbs) for any of the words in my sentences?

Publishing

At last! You've gone over your report with an eagle eye, correcting all errors and polishing every sentence until it shines. Now you are ready to complete the last step in the writing process: publishing your report.

There are many different ways to publish your writing. Right now, we'll concentrate on traditional, handwritten or typed (or computer-printed) reports on paper. Later in this chapter we'll talk a little bit about some other ways of publishing your reports.

Publishing a Traditional Report

You've reached the point in the writing process when neatness counts. When you've finished the revision process, you will handwrite or type (on a typewriter or computer) your report on sheets of paper. If handwriting, use lined paper, skipping a space between each line of writing, especially if your handwriting is small. After all, your teacher has to read a lot of reports, and after a while, teachers' eyes start to hurt! You want to be sure your teacher can read every word you've taken so much care to write. (Check with your teacher to make sure he or she wants you to skip a space between each line you write.)

You might want to include charts, diagrams, illustrations, or photos in your report. If so, make sure to include them as closely as possible to the spot in the text where you've written about them.

In the last chapter, we looked at paragraphs that had to do with Egyptian shipbuilding. If you were writing a report on that topic, and you like to draw, you might want to draw a picture of an Egyptian ship and label the different parts that your report describes. Or, if the research book where you found your information was illustrated with pictures or photos of Egyptian artifacts, you might want to make a photocopy of the illustration and paste it into your report. But be sure to give credit to the book where you got the illustration, just as you would give credit to a person whose words you quoted. A picture that someone else drew is like a quote that is drawn instead of spoken.

When you do insert charts, diagrams, or illustrations, make sure you label them so your teacher knows why you've inserted them. For example:

Egyptian ship showing the battering ram on the front.

These labels are sometimes called captions. Look through textbooks, newspapers, magazines, and research books such as encyclopedias to get an idea of how to write good captions. You will see them under photos, diagrams, illustrations, and charts. Use them as models for your own writing.

Credit Where Credit Is Due

Footnotes also add an important element to your report. As the name indicates, a footnote is a note that goes at the foot, or bottom, of the page. As you recall, you can include some information from another speaker or author in your report, as long as you make sure to set it off from your own words by using quotation marks and giving the original speaker or author credit. Using footnotes is another way to give credit. In a footnote, you can indicate where you found the quotation you used.

The first quote in your report will be footnote number 1. After you complete writing the quote, write a small number 1, like so:

> After a while it seemed to Tom that he had been sitting long enough to hatch at least one. He got off the nest with great care. All six eggs were just as they had been.[1]

Then, at the bottom of the page (you will have to leave room to do this), put another number 1, and next to it write the publishing information that you will find on the copyright page of the book in which you found the quote. A footnote containing publishing information for the above quote looks like this:

1. From *Thomas A. Edison: Young Inventor,* by Sue Guthridge, 1947, 1959, 1983, 1986, Aladdin Paperbacks, New York, NY.

Notice that the title of the book used is in italics (or underlined, if you handwrite your report), the author's name is spelled out, and the copyright date, the publisher's name, and the city where the publisher is located are included. This information is all found on the copyright page of every published book, which is usually right inside the front cover, within the first page or two.

Publishing information for newspapers or magazines is usually somewhere in the beginning of the publication (within the first five or ten pages). You may have to search for it.

A footnote containing publishing information for a newspaper looks like this:

1. From "John Glenn's Experiments to Provide Valuable Information," *The Daily Gazette,* November 3, 1998.

Notice that the title of the article from which the information came is in quotation marks, with a comma inside the ending quotation mark; the title of the newspaper or magazine is in italics (again, underlined if you are handwriting your report); and instead of the city where the newspaper or magazine is published, the issue date of the publication (which you can find on the front cover) is included.

Some publications, usually magazines, also have a volume and an issue number. If they do, you should include that information after the date:

1. From "You Can Stop Beach Erosion," *Our Environment,* June 14, 1998, Volume 3, Issue 6.

100 • Publishing

If you took your information from the Internet or from a CD-ROM, list the Web site or CD-ROM in your footnote. A Web-site footnote looks like this:

1. From the Nevada Power Web site, www.nevadapower.com.

A CD-ROM footnote looks like this:

1. *History Quick.* Jamaica, NY: Punkydoodle Software, Inc. (8806 Parsons Blvd., 11432). IBM and Mac compatible.

Sometimes your teacher will ask you to include a bibliography with your report. A bibliography is similar to footnotes in that it tells where you found the information you used in preparing your report. However, instead of listing the information at the bottom of the page where your quoted information appears, a bibliography lists the research materials all in one place at the end of your report.

When writing your report, you won't necessarily use direct quotes from all of your research materials in the body of your report. Sometimes you just take the information you learned from your research and restate it in your own words. In that case, you wouldn't need to use footnotes, but you would still need to create a bibliography to tell where you got the information on which you based sentences in your report.

Another difference between these two types of citations is that in a footnote, the name of the book, newspaper, or other resource comes first. In a bibliography, the name of the author or editor comes first, as you will see in the example on the next page.

Whether you use footnotes or not, you can still include a bibliography. And sometimes a teacher requires that you include one. So it's good to learn how to prepare one. There are several different ways to write bibliographies; one good way is shown below.

What a Bibliography Looks Like

A bibliography comes at the very end of your report, after the last sentence you have written. You can start it on a new page, or, if you have room at the bottom of the last page of your writing, you can skip a few spaces and begin your bibliography there. Start by titling it "Bibliography."

Under this heading, list the materials you used to prepare your report. If you used a combination of books, maga-

Bibliography

Books
Cavell, Juno. (1980). *Mammals I Have Known.* Henderson, NV: Bo Publications.
Messina, Cynthia. (1992). *Be Kind to Animals.* Atlantic City, NJ: Pageant Publishing.
Schmidt, Pattie M. (1970). *All About Hamsters.* Hillcrest, NY: Highland Avenue Publishers.

Magazines and Newspapers
Animal News. Volume 5, Issue 4. April, 1996. "Don't Have Your Pet's Ears Pierced." (Sunnyvale, CA)
Daily Pet Journal. July 4, 1997. "Local Shelter Saves the Day." (Las Vegas, NV)

Software and Internet Sites
Animal World. Petaluma, CA. Pawprint Software, Inc. (2345 S. Cornelius Street). IBM and Mac versions
Division of Mammals.
   http://www.nmnh.si.edu/vert/mammals/mammals.html

zines, newspapers, and computer resources (software like CD-ROMs and Internet sites), you might want to divide your bibliography into sections. Whether you break your bibliography into sections or not, list the materials you used in alphabetical order.

If you took your research notes on a grid, writing down the publication information in the separate boxes, you should have no problem transferring that information into your bibliography.

The techniques described above are all used when preparing traditional reports. But what do you do when your teacher has assigned an unusual kind of report?

Different Ways to Present Reports

Your teacher may sometimes assign you to create a report in a format that's very different from the traditional one we've been discussing throughout this book. In this case, you may still be asked to do research, take notes,

Some other written formats you might use to create your report are:

poetry	newspaper stories
journals/diaries	interviews
letters	radio or television scripts
cartoons/comic strips	plays (reader's theater)
brochures	

Some non-written formats you might use include:

models	time lines
graphs	filmstrips
videos	costumes
dolls/puppets	artwork (illustrations, sculptures, etc.)
dioramas	maps

and make yourself an expert on some topic. But instead of having you write about that topic, your teacher may ask you to convey your information in the form of artwork, or a poem, or any number of other formats.

Many of these formats need no explanation. However, there are a few that you might find a little challenging. We'll look at some of the unusual formats here. (Oral reports or presentations are another way to present your research. We'll talk about them in the next chapter.)

Journals

If you were creating a report on the Civil War, one interesting way to present the report might be in the form of a journal. You could pretend to be a student at the time of the Civil War, a farm worker, a soldier, a woman waiting for her husband to return from battle, or a slave fighting to be free.

Remember that a journal is supposed to be a daily record similar to a diary, so write in "day-long" sections, and use descriptive words that would be appropriate for the period you are writing about. If you are writing about the Civil War, your character *wouldn't* say, "I spent the evening watching television." Television hadn't been invented yet!

Using the notes you have collected from your research, you might write an "eyewitness" account of a battle, or tell about the hard times experienced by the families left at home while the soldiers went off to fight.

Cartoons, Comic Strips

Cartoons and comic strips are great ways to recount events in history or tell about a person or civilization. You are probably already very familiar with comic strips and don't need help in figuring out how to illustrate one. If not, check the comic strips in the Sunday edition of your local paper for examples. Remember to leave enough room to write dialogue in word balloons and narration in boxes at the top or bottom of each frame.

Brochures

In some schools students spend a year studying their own state's history and geography. If this is the case in your school, and you are about to do a report on this subject, a good way to present the information is in the form of a travel brochure. One way to get ideas is to ask a local travel agent for some sample brochures and then model yours after them.

These are only a few alternative report formats. The others are not described in depth here because either they are easier to figure out yourself, or they require more instruction than we can cover here. However, you might want to show this list to your teacher and ask for his or her ideas about using some of them. He or she may suggest using a combination of formats—perhaps a written report with a graph or illustrated map. Your teacher might even come up with some other unique ideas that can make presenting research reports seem more like fun than schoolwork.

Publishing Your Reports

Ask yourself these questions when you're ready to hand in your report:

- ❏ Are my lines spaced at least one and a half spaces apart so the report can be read easily?
- ❏ If this report is handwritten, is my handwriting neat and easy to read?
- ❏ Is my report clean, with no food or drink stains on the paper? (Reports should have neat handwriting and no stains.)
- ❏ If there are footnotes, are they formatted correctly and numbered in the right order?
- ❏ Have I prepared a bibliography to show my research materials?
- ❏ Are my bibliography entries listed in alphabetical order?
- ❏ Are my bibliography entries written correctly? (Check the guidelines on page 101.)

Oral Reports

Would you believe that researchers have found that the majority of adults are more afraid of speaking in public than they are of dying? It's true: The thought of giving a speech or making an oral presentation simply petrifies them. Yet in school, students are often required to make oral presentations. And although for some it may not be their favorite school activity, it's still one they manage to get through without too much trouble. (Maybe adults are just not as courageous as young people? Hhhhmmmmm . . . sounds like a topic for a research report!)

Oral reports don't have to be frightening to people of any age. In fact, they can be fun—especially if your teacher encourages or allows you to get into the spirit of the report, maybe even dressing up "in character" to get your audience's attention. Oral reports can really be enjoyable, both for you and for your audience. If you are a person who enjoys acting, singing, or other forms of performance, then oral reports will probably become your favorites.

How to Prepare an Oral Report

A good oral report should start out in almost exactly the same way as a written report. This means starting at the beginning of the writing process and brainstorming a topic, collecting details, taking

Oral Reports • 107

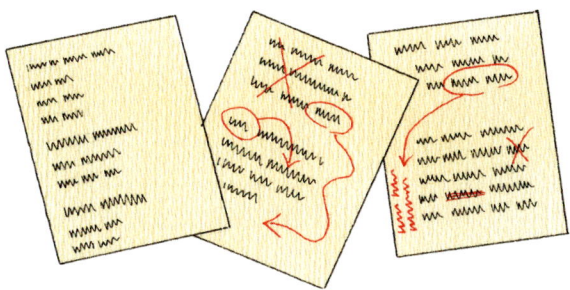

notes, making an outline, creating a rough draft, and including a bibliography.

Did you notice the one step of the writing process that was not listed in the last paragraph? The final step of revising, editing, and proofreading your rough draft is usually not necessary when preparing an oral report, because there is no final draft. Or, it might be more accurate to say that your speech is the final draft, and when you speak, of course, spelling and neatness don't apply. (Unless your teacher wants you to hand in your speech notes after you present your report. In that case, you'll need to prepare a neat and correctly written report as well.)

The one part of your report that you will probably need to polish, making sure all the information is correct and everything is spelled correctly and written neatly, is the bibliography. Even if your teacher does not require you to hand in a copy of your written report when you present your oral report, he or she may want you to show the results of your research in some way, and a bibliography is one way to do that.

There is a form of revising that you definitely need to perform when creating an oral report. You need to practice delivering the report, either to an audience (parents are

always good) or to a tape recorder.

If you have the kind of parents who always think everything you do is great, they might not be "tough enough" on you. You might want to find someone else to practice in front of—someone who will give you honest, constructive criticism that will help you improve your delivery. On the other hand, if your parents are overly critical, they might get you too discouraged with their well-meaning comments.

Dos and Don'ts of Criticism

• Criticize in a positive way. Don't just say things like: "I don't like..." or "You made a mistake when..." Instead, express your criticism in positive terms by saying things like: "You might want to think about changing..." or, "Can you think of a better way to say...?"

• Always try to blend a positive suggestion with a criticism to make it easier for your partner to correct mistakes. For example: "I really like your topic, but when you speak so quickly I find it hard to keep track of all the facts. Maybe you could try speaking a little more slowly."

• Use the "sandwich" method: When you notice a mistake or have a criticism to make, soften the sting for your partner by making your criticism the "filling" in a sandwich that has "bread" made of compliments. For example:

"I really liked the way you paused between words. It made it easy to understand what you were saying." (compliment)

"One thing you might work on is trying not to giggle so much." (criticism)

"But I wouldn't change the way you pause between words. It's really very good." (compliment)

In that case, you might be better off with a friend or school buddy as a practice audience. You are the best judge of your own situation. But getting some kind of feedback before the official delivery of the report will help, so it's worth trying to find the right audience to practice in front of.

It can be a good idea to ask a school friend to partner with you so you can give each other feedback on your reports, especially if your teacher has assigned oral reports to the entire class. Working together will give each of you the help you need to turn your rough reports into polished gems. But when you and your partner give feedback to each other, remember The Golden Rule: "Do unto others as you would have others do unto you." That means it's okay to offer constructive criticism that will help your partner correct mistakes and make improvements—but do it with kindness, the way you would want your partner to critique you.

The Delivery

Some things you should try to do when practicing and, ultimately, delivering, your oral report are listed below.

➤ Speak loudly and clearly. Even if you have to slow down until your words sound like they're being spoken too slowly to your own ear, it's probably better than rushing through your speech.

➤ Speak with expression. If you're speaking about an Arctic explorer and you're describing the freezing hardships she endured, make your voice shake like you're shivering. If your topic is something happy or pleasant, smile when you speak about it. Even if people can't see your face, they can "hear" a smile in your voice. But if your topic is tragic, it wouldn't be appropriate to deliver your report with a big smile on your face. Match your expression to your topic and you can't go wrong. (For an example of speaking with expression, watch your local TV news. Those anchor men and women smile when they report on happy stories, and put sadness into their voices and facial expressions when the story is sad. You can do the same when delivering your speeches.)

➤ Make eye contact with your audience. Don't just deliver your speech to the floor or keep your eyes glued to the clock on the wall in the back of the room when you speak. Make believe your head is a camera, and that you are taking movies of the entire class. Start at the door and sweep across the classroom to the windows, s-l-o-w-l-y, stopping to look at the faces of your classmates and teacher as you turn your head a little. If you feel too shy to make eye contact, at least make "chin" contact: As you turn your head, look at some part of the face of a student in each row. The other observers in the audience will think you are making eye contact.

Remember, no one but you knows how badly your knees are knocking. It's true! Even though your knees feel like they're jumping around or ready to collapse, no one can notice them but you, especially if you're wearing long pants. And if your teacher has allowed you to get dressed in a costume

HANDY TIP:

If you get nervous while delivering your speech, some professional speakers recommend imagining your audience sitting in their underwear. It's hard to feel nervous in front of a crowd of people dressed like that.

It might, however, be more practical to practice taking a few deep breaths through your nose, with the tip of your tongue pressed against the spot where your front teeth and your gums meet. Breathe in slowly, and out again slowly, being careful not to make yourself dizzy. Deep breathing exercises are a good way to relax and get your lungs the oxygen they need to help your words come out loud and clear.

to deliver your speech, you can disguise the knocking altogether by making sure your costume covers your legs entirely!

➤ If you are not planning to memorize your report, but are planning to read it from your paper, make sure you do not hold the paper in front of your face. It's tempting to try to hide from the rest of the class, especially if you are a little shy. But putting your paper in front of your face will only make it more difficult for everyone, including your teacher, to hear you. So bite the bullet and put the paper down. Better yet, memorize your report so you don't have to read it from the page. If you do memorize it, it is a good idea to write down key words or topic sentences from your outline onto index cards. Glance briefly at the cards to remind yourself what comes next. If you are nervous, this can prevent you from panicking and forgetting your speech!

➤ Sitting or standing, *be still!* Do not weave or sway back and forth. Try to be conscious of standing still. Use your arms to make gestures, of course, but don't let your body sway back and forth. One way to prevent yourself from swaying is to put your heels together and keep them together while you speak.

➤ Focus on your report. Never mind that the American flag in the corner of the room is blowing in the breeze and touching the bulletin board. Ignore it. Ignore the class pet in its cage on the shelf. Ignore the water dripping from the classroom sink, and the kid in the third row who's biting his nails. Just concentrate on your topic.

➤ Don't become a "Wizard of Ahs." Try to be conscious of the number of times you say "um" and "ah." If you are able to tape record yourself before delivering your speech in front of your class, you might be surprised how many "ums" and "ahs" you hear yourself utter. One way to correct this is to try counting the number of "ums" and "ahs" when you first play the tape back for yourself, then try recording yourself again and again, making a conscious effort to reduce the number of "ums" and "ahs" each time. These are speech habits almost everyone has, and almost no one is aware of them until it's time to give an oral report. These little noises can distract listeners from hearing your message, so it's worth it to try to get rid of them. Fortunately, with a little effort, it can be done.

➤ Don't worry if you make mistakes. No one is perfect. Someone once asked Thomas Edison, the inventor of the lightbulb, if he felt bad about the large number of failures he'd had before his invention was perfected. He had tried 50,000 experiments before his lightbulb was a success. He didn't feel bad about his failures, though. He looked at his mistakes as an opportunity to learn, not as things to feel bad about. So don't worry if your report isn't delivered perfectly. Just try your best, and use the suggestions here to help you.

Delivering an Oral Report

When practicing my oral report, did I:

- ❏ speak loudly enough to be heard?
- ❏ speak clearly enough to be understood?
- ❏ speak slowly to avoid rushing?
- ❏ speak with expression?
- ❏ make eye contact with my audience?
- ❏ refer to my notes only when necessary?
- ❏ hold my notes low, not in front of my face?
- ❏ sit or stand up straight?
- ❏ put my heels together and remember not to sway?
- ❏ focus on my speech, not on what's going on around me?

Summary

Well, there you have it: the rules for creating top-notch reports. By following the suggestions outlined in this book, you should be able to create great reports on any topic. We've covered all the bases, from brainstorming a topic to publishing a flawless written report or delivering a polished oral report. Let's review briefly.

First, (if your teacher does not assign a topic) select a topic.

Next, brainstorm details about the topic to research. Jot the details down on paper in the form of a web or list, or in whatever way suits your learning style.

Use reference materials such as books, magazines, videos, CD-ROMs, the Internet, and so on, to find facts about your topic.

Write notes about your facts on a note-taking grid or by listing them in a web or whatever other way suits your learning style.

Using your facts, create an outline that lists everything you want to include in your report.

Using your outline, write an introductory paragraph, body paragraphs, and a concluding paragraph for your report.

Using the rough draft you have written, polish your report by revising it: edit, proofread, and copy it over again neatly, either by hand, computer, or typewriter, correcting any mistakes as you go.

If you are doing an oral report, practice until you can deliver it smoothly, without relying on your notes too much.

Learning to do research, take notes, and write good reports is a skill set that will serve you well throughout the rest of your life. Whether you plan to go on to college or to go directly into the world of work, learning how to create well-organized, polished reports is something everyone needs to know. It's a skill that makes you stand out. The lessons in this book will help you do that.

Appendix

Quotes and Sayings You Can Use for Inspiration or in Introductory Paragraphs

These quotations—and many others you can find in a variety of books, magazines such as *Reader's Digest,* and on Internet sites (type in keyword <quotes> when doing a search)—can be especially useful if you are asked to write a report that gives your opinion. Whatever your opinion is of a subject, you can find a quote to support it. There are many excellent collections of quotations in your local library; those listed here will get you started.

When you can do the common things of life in an uncommon way, you will command the attention of the world.

—*George Washington Carver*

The above quote might be used to begin a report about an inventor or a performer with a unique talent.

If you can walk, you can dance. If you can talk, you can sing.

—*African proverb*

The above quote might be used to begin a report about gaining the confidence to try something new, or building on what one already knows to achieve a new goal.

A smile breaks down most barriers.

—*anonymous*

This quote could begin a report on the importance of being positive in all your dealings with people.

Your time may be limited, but your imagination is not.
—*anonymous*

This would be a good quote to use in a report about an inventor, an artist, a performer, or another person who is creative.

Actions speak louder than words.
—*anonymous*

The above quote might be used to begin a report about a person who accomplished a great deal by his or her actions. Or you might use it to begin a report that gives your opinion about whether the quote is true or not. Support your opinion with facts.

**The world is so full of a number of things,
I'm sure we should all be as happy as kings.**
—*Robert Louis Stevenson, Scottish poet*

The above quote might be used to begin a report about the importance of appreciating the world around us, or a report about specific features of nature that make us happy, like sunshine, trees, fresh air, clean water, and so on.

A wise person turns stumbling blocks into stepping stones.
—*anonymous*

This quote might also be used to begin a report about a person who overcame obstacles to achieve success.

To achieve it, you must first believe it.
—anonymous

The above quote might be used to begin a report about the importance of setting goals and believing in one's self. It might also be used to begin a report on a historical character who overcame obstacles by believing in herself or himself.

You can't hurt your eyesight looking at the bright side of life.
—anonymous

This quote might be used to begin a report on the importance of keeping a positive outlook in life.

No pain, no gain.
—American proverb

This quote might be used to begin a report on an athlete or other achiever who made sacrifices but who ultimately achieved success.

The most beautiful thing in the world is freedom of speech.
—Diogenes, Greek philosopher

This quote might be used in a report that gives your opinion. Do you agree with the quote or not? Are there historical or current events in the news that influenced your opinion?

When one door shuts, another opens.
—proverb

This quote might begin a report on a personal experience you've had where one opportunity was denied you, but another came your way.

Imagination is more important than knowledge.
—*Albert Einstein*

Do you agree? Use this quote in an opinion report.

The strongest man in the world is he who stands alone.
—*Henrik Ibsen, Norwegian playwright*

This quote might start a report about a historical figure who stood alone against opponents, yet succeeded in reaching his or her goal.

Every individual has a place to fill in the world, and is important, in some respect, whether he chooses to be so or not.
—*Nathaniel Hawthorne, American writer*

This quote might begin a report on a historical figure who started life as an unimportant person and rose to play an important role in history.

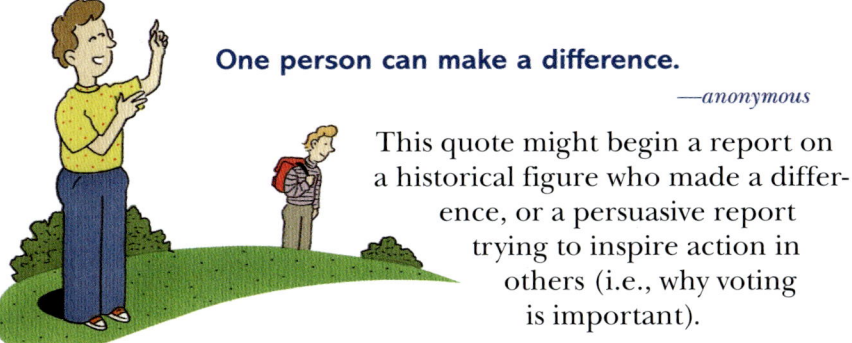

One person can make a difference.
—*anonymous*

This quote might begin a report on a historical figure who made a difference, or a persuasive report trying to inspire action in others (i.e., why voting is important).

A man cannot be comfortable without his own approval.
—*Mark Twain, American writer and humorist*

What do you suppose Mark Twain meant by this quote? This might be a good beginning for a humorous report on what it means to "have your own approval."

118 • Appendix

Some people count time, others make time count.
—*proverb*

What do you think this quote means? Can you think of examples of each type of person the quote speaks about?

One kind word can warm three winter months.
—*Japanese proverb*

What do you think this quote means? It might start an opinion report.

It's always right to vote for the best man, but the chances are that the best man is not running.
—*anonymous*

This might be a good quote to use in a report on local or national elections that are in the news, or on elections for schoolwide offices.

An integral part of being a star is having the will to win. All the champions have it.
—*Betty Cuthbert, Australian Olympic gold-medal sprinter*

Shoot for the moon. Even if you miss it, you'll land among the stars.
—*Les Brown, American journalist*

The world stands aside to let anyone pass who knows where he is going.
—*David Starr Jordan, American educator*

These three quotes would be useful in writing about a champion of some kind.

The trouble with this country is that there are too many people going about saying, "The trouble with this country is..."
—*Sinclair Lewis*

Do you agree or disagree? This might make a funny quote to begin a report on "The trouble with this country..."

Whoever walks with the wise becomes wise.
—*Proverbs 13:20*

What do you think this quote means? This might be a good start for a report that gives advice on the importance of choosing friends wisely.

The miracles of nature are all around us.
—*anonymous*

This quote also might start an opinion report. Or it can be used as a creative opening for a descriptive report about a unique animal or plant.

If there be righteousness in the heart, there will be beauty in the character.

If there be beauty in the character, there will be harmony in the home.

If there be harmony in the home, there will be order in the nation.

If there be order in the nation, there will be peace in the world.
—*Confucius, Chinese philosopher*

What do you think of this quote? Do you agree or disagree with Confucius? Can you give examples?

You are not in charge of the Universe: You are in charge of yourself.

—*Arnold Bennett*

Some people want to change the world; others are more interested in improving themselves. Use this quote to begin an essay comparing and contrasting two historical characters, one who changed the world, one who changed his or her own life. Which kind of person would you rather be?

Success consists of getting up just one more time than you fall.

—*Oliver Goldsmith, British author*

Until you try, you don't know what you can do.

—*Henry James, American novelist*

The two quotes above might be used to begin a report on the importance of making an effort. You might report on an experience you've had that demonstrates the truth of these sayings, or about someone else who succeeded after facing the fear of failure.

Responsibility is the price every man must pay for freedom.

—*Edith Hamilton*

Use this quote to begin a report on men or women who have shouldered responsibility to pay for freedom, such as freedom fighters.

Nonviolence is the first article of my faith.

—*Mahatma Gandhi*

This quote could be used to begin a report on Dr. Martin Luther King., Jr.; or on Gandhi himself, who inspired Dr. King; or to introduce a report on the American Civil Rights movement; or any other examples of people who changed the world by nonviolent means.

Science has promised us truth. It has never promised us either peace or happiness.

—*Gustave LeBon*

Science has given us many ways to improve and extend our lives, but it has also given us many tools to destroy life, such as more powerful weapons. This is a perfect quote to introduce a report on the benefits and drawbacks of scientific and technological progress.

There are two tragedies in life. One is to lose your heart's desire. The other is to gain it.

—*George Bernard Shaw*

This kind of quote is called a "paradox." It's almost a puzzle. Can you think about what it might mean and write a report on what you think George Bernard Shaw was talking about? Can you give examples of ways that getting one's heart's desire and losing it might both be tragic?

Don't start living tomorrow—tomorrow never arrives. Start working on your dreams and ambitions today.

—*anonymous*

The bud of a rose is just as beautiful as the full bloom. Appreciate what you have at the moment.

—*anonymous*

Do you agree or disagree? These quotes could be a good starting point for a report based on your opinion.

Glossary

apostrophe
The superscript sign (') used to indicate the omission of a letter or letters from a word, or to indicate the possessive case.

appendix
A collection of supplementary material, usually found at the end of a book.

bibliography
A list of sources used or considered by an author in preparing a particular work.

brainstorming
The process of trying to get ideas out on paper. The creation of a sudden clever plan or idea.

contraction
A new word made by combining two whole words, leaving out one or more letters in between and replacing the missing letters with an apostrophe (e.g., do not = don't, has not = hasn't).

fact
A statement that can be verified and proven by using the scientific method or other reliable evidence, such as documentation or eye-witness testimony. Facts are necessary to prove a point.

footnote
A numbered note of explanation located at the bottom of a page of text. It refers to a word or phrase in the body of the text that is marked with the same number.

homophone
A word that sounds exactly like another word that has a different meaning. Both words are usually spelled differently, however (e.g., hear, here).

indefinite pronouns
Pronouns that do not refer to a specific person, place, or thing, but to one or more persons, places, or things that are not specified. Indefinite pronouns can be singular or plural in number (e.g., any, all, none).

Internet
An interconnecting system of computer sites that is accessible from a user's personal computer (providing the computer is equipped with a program that allows it to connect to the Internet).

italics
A style of printing type patterned on a Renaissance script with the letters slanting to the right. This is the accepted typeface used for titles of books, shows, and periodicals in printed materials.

metaphor
A figure of speech in which a word or phrase that ordinarily indicates one thing is used to indicate another, making an implicit comparison (e.g., a sea of troubles). Metaphors do not contain the words "like" or "as."

noun
A word that names a person, place, or thing.

opinion
A belief or conclusion held confidently but not necessarily proven by facts or positive knowledge.

plural
A noun that represents more than one person, place, or thing, or a verb that indicates action or being performed by more than one person, place, or thing. Subjects and verbs in sentences must always agree in "number."

punctuation
The use of standard marks and signs in writing and printing to separate words into sentences, clauses, and phrases in order to clarify meaning.

revision
The act or process of improving, changing, and correcting written material. It's part of the writing process.

sentence fragment
A group of words that begins with a capital letter and ends with a period, question mark, or exclamation mark, but does not contain both a subject and a verb. It is not a complete sentence.

sequential outline
A way of organizing data that indicates the order in which events took place: a time line.

simile
A comparison between two objects using the words "like" or "as" (e.g., the baby's cheek was as soft as a rose petal).

singular
One person, place, or thing; or a verb that describes the action or being of a single entity.

synonym
A word having the same or nearly the same meaning as another word or other words (e.g., child, kid, youngster).

topic
The subject of a sentence, essay, paragraph, or report. This is the main thing that is being discussed, described, or explained.

Venn diagram
A diagram composed of two overlapping circles that is often used to compare and contrast information.

verb
A word that shows action or being. It is a necessary part of every sentence.

writing process
A model for writing that includes a number of steps, such as choosing a topic, brainstorming details, collecting data/doing research, writing a first draft, revising the draft to create a final copy, and "publishing" the report by sharing it in written or oral format with an audience.

Index

A
adjectives
  capitalization of, 87–88
  defined, 63
adverbs, 63
apostrophes, 81
appendix, defined, 24
articles, 88–89
artwork, in reports, 97–98
audience, 18–20, 52

B
bibliography
  defined, 24
  preparing, 100–102
body paragraphs
  checklist for, 68
  defined, 7, 65
  writing, 65–68
brochures, 104

C
capitalization
  of proper adjectives, 87–88
  of proper nouns, 59, 87
  of report titles, 88–89
captions, 97–98
cartoons, 104
charts, 16–17
checklists
  body, 68
  conclusion, 72

checklists *(continued)*
  editing and proofreading, 95
  introduction, 64
  oral report, 112
  publishing, 105
  research, 29
  revision, 77
  using, 10
  writing process, 10, 20
chronological report outlines, 41, 43
comic strips, 104
common nouns, 59
comparison/contrast reports
  note-taking grids for, 38
  outlines for, 44–45
  writing purpose and, 19
concept outlines, 48
conclusion
  checklist for, 72
  defined, 7, 69
  topic sentence in, 71–72
  writing, 69–72
contractions, 81
copyright page, defined, 24
criticism, 108–109

D
definitions, 122–124
descriptive report outlines, 41–42
direct quotations, 32, 89–91
drafting. *See* rough draft.

E

editing and proofreading
　capitalization, 87–89
　checklist for, 95
　defined, 8–9
　indefinite pronouns, 86
　marks for, 93–95
　punctuation, 79, 82–83
　quotations, 89–91
　spelling, 78–81
　subject-verb agreement, 83–85
　titles of works of art, 91–92
entertaining writing, 17–18
events, as supporting details, 23–24
examples, defined, 23
exclamation mark, 82
eye contact, during oral reports, 110

F

facial expression, during oral reports, 109–110
facts, defined, 21
fear, of oral reports, 106, 110
Five Ws and H, 33–36
flow-chart outlines, 49
footnotes, 98–100

G

glossary, defined, 24
grid, note-taking, 36–40

H

homophones, 80

I

ideas
　developing, 13–17
　sources for, 11–13
illustrations, 97–98
indefinite pronouns, 86
indentation, 67
index, defined, 24
informative writing, 18
In Other Words game, 31
Internet
　citation for, 100
　as research source, 27–29
interviews, 25–27
introduction
　checklist for, 64
　criteria for, 56
　defined, 6–7, 55–56
　quotations for, 114–121
　when to write, 58, 65
　writing, 56–58
its, vs. it's, 80–81

J

journals
　as idea sources, 11
　as reports, 103

L

libraries, 24
line spacing, 90, 96

M

metaphor, defined, 6

N

newspapers
　as idea sources, 12

newspapers *(continued)*
　interview questions in, 26
　as writing examples, 91
"nice," use of, 64
note taking
　direct quotations and, 32
　format for, 31
　grid for, 36–40
　paraphrasing and, 31–32
　what to include, 30–31
notes, for oral reports, 111
nouns, 59

O

opinions, defined, 21
oral reports
　checklist for, 112
　criticism of, 108–109
　delivery of, 109–112
　fear of, 106, 110
　practicing, 107–109
　preparing, 106–107
outlines
　alternative forms for, 46–51
　defined, 9, 41
　notes and, 41–42
　questions to ask about, 46
　traditional forms for, 43–45

P

paragraphs, 53–54, 66–68. *See also* specific types.
paraphrasing, 31–32
period, 82
persuasion, 38–40
possessive case, 80–81
prepositions, 88–89
prewriting, 8–9

primary sources, 25, 66
pronouns
　defined, 59–60
　indefinite, 86
proofreading. *See* editing and proofreading.
proper adjectives, 87–88
proper nouns
　capitalization of, 59, 87
　defined, 59
publishing reports
　alternative formats for, 102–105
　checklist for, 105
　defined, 8–9
　traditional format for, 96–102
punctuation, 79, 82–83, 89–90
purpose of reports, 5–6, 17–18

Q

question mark, 82
quotation marks, 89, 92
quotations
　as idea sources, 13
　note taking and, 32
　using in reports, 89–91, 114–121

R

reasons (to support opinions), defined, 21
reference materials, 24, 40
research
　checklist for, 29
　defined, 21
　as element of report, 8–10
　sources for, 24–29
　supporting details in, 21–24

revision. *See also* editing and proofreading.
   checklist for, 77
   defined, 8–9
   need for, 73
   of oral reports, 107–108
   process of, 75–76
   tips for, 76
rough draft
   of body, 65–68
   of conclusion, 69–72
   defined, 8–9
   of introduction, 52–64
   line spacing for, 90

S

search engines, 27
secondary sources, 25
sensory details, defined, 23
sentence fragments, 82–83
sentences, 53–54, 79
sentences, topic, 53, 56–58, 64, 67, 68
sequential report outlines, 41, 43, 47
simile, defined, 6
spelling, 78–81
stories, as supporting details, 23–24
subject (of sentence), understood, 61
subject-verb agreement, 83–85
summarizing, 69–70
synonyms
   for nouns, 59
   for verbs, 61–62

T

table of contents, defined, 24
textbooks, as idea sources, 13
time lines, 47
titles
   of reports, 65, 88–89
   of works cited, 91–92
"to be" verbs, 60
topic lists, 13–14
topic sentence, in conclusion, 71–72
topic sentence, in paragraphs, 53, 56–58, 64, 67, 68
topics
   developing, 13–17
   ideas for, 11–13

V

Venn diagram outlines, 50–51
verbs
   action, 60
   agreement with subjects, 83–85
   state-of-being, 60
   synonyms for, 61–62

W

Web sites. *See* Internet.
word webs, 14–15
writing process, 8–10, 20

Y

"you understood" sentences, 61